—— THERE'S ——

MORE

YOU KNOW IT ... COME AND FIND IT

SHORT ESSAYS ON JESUS' LIFE TO THE FULL

SAM HUNTER

HIGH BRIDGE
BOOKS & MEDIA

There's More
by Sam Hunter

Copyright © 2024 by Sam Hunter
All rights reserved.

Printed in the United States of America
ISBN: 978-1-962802-23-9

Unless otherwise indicated, Scripture quotations are taken from THE HOLY BIBLE, NEW INTERNATIONAL VERSION®, NIV® Copyright © 1973, 1978, 1984, 2011 by Biblica, Inc.® Used by permission. All rights reserved worldwide.

Scripture quotations marked MSG are taken from THE MESSAGE, copyright © 1993, 2002, 2018 by Eugene H. Peterson. Used by permission of NavPress. All rights reserved. Represented by Tyndale House Publishers, Inc.

Scripture quotations marked TPT are from The Passion Translation®. Copyright © 2017, 2018, 2020 by Passion & Fire Ministries, Inc. Used by permission. All rights reserved. ThePassionTranslation.com.

High Bridge Books titles may be purchased in bulk for educational, business, fundraising, or sales promotional use. For information, please contact High Bridge Books via www.HighBridgeBooks.com/contact.

Published in Houston, Texas by High Bridge Books.

This book is dedicated to my daughter, Britton, the "only girl in my life" until I married Dina, and then Britton married our much-loved Finch. She exemplifies the heart and soul of what it looks like to follow Jesus—not perfectly, but purposely and proactively and passionately in pursuit of Him. Both her fathers burst with pride over her: Her Heavenly Father and her earthly father.

Contents

Introduction

I have recently added to my email signature:

> There's more
> You know it
> Come and find … 'It'!

Here is why.

When we first started 721 Ministries twenty years ago, we did not know what we were doing, but we knew this: Men all around us were absolutely clueless – clueless on so many levels. They were well-meaning men, but missing it badly.

"The Absentee Husband and Father" became our mission field. They were not investing emotionally in their marriages, nor as fathers to their children. They did not know they were missing it. Their intentions were good. But no one was telling them, "There is so much more!"

And most critically, the scariest aspect of their clueless condition was they did not know Jesus at all. They knew about him, for the most part, but some not even that. They were getting their families to church on Sundays, and even some Wednesday night suppers. Many were serving as deacons and elders and such. But they were *Churchians*, not Christians. They were following church, not Christ.

They were in grave danger of hearing Jesus' words on Judgment Day:

> "Not everyone who says to me, 'Lord, Lord,' will enter the kingdom of heaven, but only the one who does the will of my Father who is in heaven. Many will say to

me on that day, 'Lord, Lord, did we not prophesy in your name and in your name drive out demons and in your name perform many miracles?' Then I will tell them plainly, 'I never knew you. Away from me, you evildoers!' (Matthew 7:21-23)

It was that "I never knew you" that shook me up so badly. Jesus was making this startling statement to men and women who had just listed their resumes of church activities. We made it clear, just as Jesus did, "There will be no resumes on Judgment Day."

Our calling card became, "There's more."[1] And we found that men were for the most part receptive to this. They were not offended. They knew there was something missing. They knew it! They knew there had to be more. They just did not know what the "It" was that was missing, and they sure did not know how to find it.

So we introduced them to Jesus, someone who could be their Savior – as in save them from Hell, a very real place – and also be their best friend. For twenty years I have watched Jesus change hearts, which changed lives, which changed marriages, which changed families, which changed legacies.

Now for you, reading this today, man or woman, the call is still true for you. No matter where you are in your spiritual journey, no matter how invested you are in knowing Jesus, there is always more. We can always go deeper. And the riches that await are immeasurable.

So I close with these beautiful words of scripture, because our 721 call echoes these calls from the Father and from Jesus:

This is what the Lord says:
"Stand at the crossroads and look;
    ask for the ancient paths,
ask where the good way is, and walk in it,
    and you will find rest for your souls. (Jer. 6:16,
    bold added)

"Come to me, all you who are weary and burdened, and I will give you rest. Take my yoke upon you and learn from me, for I am gentle and humble in heart, **and you will find rest for your souls**. For my yoke is easy and my burden is light." (Matt. 11:28-30, bold added)

Rest for your souls.
There's more.
You know it.
Come and find it.

---

[1] Det Bowers

Part 1

Surrender

1

To Clean Up, Trust Up

An excerpt from Peter in
The Missing Link

I remember the day Jesus accepted an invitation from a Pharisee to have dinner. Not all of the Pharisees were out to get Jesus, and this man, Jonah, seemed genuinely interested in this new young rabbi. As a matter of fact, he had been a business partner with Ananias. He was not a bad man, but he was nevertheless obsessed with the details of the Law. I could see Jonah was surprised when he noticed that Jesus did not first wash before the meal, and he said so.

I was watching Jesus, and I could see he had already sized up this man's heart. Jesus knew he was focused on his public performance, as well as his possessions, so he said to him, "Now then, you Pharisees clean the outside of the cup and dish, but inside you are full of greed and wickedness. But give what is inside the dish to the poor, and everything will be clean for you."

I have to admit I was surprised by Jesus' words. I wasn't surprised by Jesus' abrupt challenge, he had a way of cutting right to the point. But to my way of thinking Jesus should say something like, "You should clean the inside of the dish, like you do the outside."

This man was squeaky clean on the outside; he seemed to do everything right and was very religious. I expected Jesus to tell this man to get his heart right, and to stop being so obsessed with his outsides, and start focusing on his insides.

Why then did he say, "Give what is inside to the poor?" For that matter, why did he tell the young ruler to give it all away? What does giving have to do with cleaning our insides? The answer has become obvious as the Holy Spirit has given me more clarity: Jesus knows our hearts, and he knows nothing competes for our hearts more than our … money.

Our possessions too often possess us, and keep us in a prison of possession.

So in all cases, Jesus knows the quickest way to start the process of surrendering to him is to start the process of trusting him. And nothing will force you to trust him more than to obey his commands to give, and give generously.

2

Pasture

Imagine if you lived in Jesus' real world, the one he de- scribes with images of beautiful green pastures. Jesus describes what life in his very real Kingdom is like with his picture of a quiet and serene, nourishing pasture: "I am the gate; whoever enters through me will be saved. He will come in and go out, and find pasture."

"He will come in and go out, and find pasture." Jesus is saying that life in his Kingdom is a life of relaxing, rhythmic balance. No matter where or what the circumstances, whether "going in" his protective and comforting presence, or "going out" in our *real* world, we will find pasture.

Pasture.

King David painted this same picture in his beautiful shepherd psalm:

> "The LORD is my shepherd, I shall not be in want. He makes me lie down in green pastures, he leads me beside quiet waters, he restores my soul."

Green pastures. Quiet waters. He restores my soul: Soul restoration. I want this, don't you?

"But you don't understand my life," I've had people say to me, both men and women. "If I don't, it won't! If I don't push, control, manipulate, force, fix … it, or them, it won't go the way it has to for me to be happy."

Green pastures. Quiet waters. Soul restoration. Life in his Kingdom.

"But what about my boss? What about my child, who is not doing right? What about my spouse, whom I can't seem to fix? For crying out loud, what about Rome? Don't give me your platitudes about God and Jesus. Try living in my world – the real world."

To which Jesus might say, "The thief comes only to steal and kill and destroy; I have come that they may have life, and have it to the full."

You can have this life, my friend. It's not a sales pitch from Jesus. He means it. It's real. It's available. You can have it. But you can't have it with your, "If I don't, it won't," approach to life. You can't have it with your busy, harried, more-is-better life.

And you cannot have it trusting Self over God. The Self-life will steal your peace. Self leads only to the empty life, the average life, even the substandard life. Life to the full, the true life that is truly life, is only open to you through trust.

Trust.

Trust he is for you, he is with you, and he is even out before you.

Green pastures. Quiet waters. Soul restoration.

This is Life in the Kingdom of God.

3

Follow Me

We've been talking about what it looks like to have a personal relationship with Jesus, and through this personal relationship to grow to know God as your heavenly Father. *Your* heavenly Father. Personal. Intimate. Real. Jesus promises to show you the way into this relationship, as well as to show you the way to having him as your best friend.

Perhaps you thought the way was trying so very hard to follow all the rules, but Jesus' invitation is, "Follow me," not, "Follow my rules."

I was walking around downtown Greenville recently and a Canadian couple approached me asking for directions. I knew exactly how to tell them the way to their destination, but I quickly realized that even though it wasn't complicated, it would *sound* complicated. So I simply said, "Just follow me and I'll show you the way."

This is Jesus' invitation to you, and his promise to do the same for you. On his last night with his disciples, Jesus said, "You know the way to the place I am going." Philip, speaking for all of us, responded with, "Lord, we don't know where you are going, so how can we know the way?"

To which Jesus said, "Don't you remember all I taught you, Philip? Shame on you. Go back and study your notes from my Sermon on the Mount. And here's my lecture outline on "12 Steps to Finding the Way."

No, Jesus actually answered, "I am the way and the truth and the life. ... If you really knew me, you would know my Father as well." (John 14:4-7)

"I am the way. Follow me." Simple. Direct. Easy to understand. But gosh we make it complicated, don't we? We get distracted by all kinds of "What about?" and "What if?" questions, and worries about anything and everything, except the only thing ... person that matters. People distract us. Denominations distract us. Other Christian's behavior distracts us. Doctrine and theology distract us.

The apostle Peter had this distraction issue throughout the time he followed Jesus:

Peter and Jesus are walking down the beach together. It is after the resurrection, which means Peter has seen Jesus dead and buried, and has since seen him alive, several times. One might think this would simplify things for Peter.

And for us as well. But Peter is distracted by another disciple following them. So he says, "Lord, what about him?" That's us! "What about? What if?" Jesus' answer to Peter is his same answer to you and to me: " ...what is that to you? *You* must follow me." (John 21:21-22 italics added)

"You must follow me." You ... as in you, my friend, must follow Jesus – personally, individually. Not follow your church, your small group leader, and certainly not the culture. And all those distractions? "What's that to you? You must follow me."

May you focus on following Jesus, not following rules. Because there is nothing personal nor powerful about rules without a relationship.

4

The Hardest Thing

The Holy Spirit guides and directs us with green, yellow, and red lights, step by step. But there is one thing the Holy Spirit directs us to do that is perhaps the hardest of all: to wait.

It is perhaps the hardest thing for us busy, can-do, "If-I-don't-it-won't" Americans to do. The complications we usher into our lives from ignoring this guidance from Holy Spirit could so easily be avoided and are oh so messy when we don't. Just think of the problems that would have been avoided if Adam had said to Eve, "I know the fruit looks delicious, and maybe the serpent is right that we did hear God wrong, but why don't we just wait and ask God?"

But I don't like to wait. I've got to act now! Waiting means I might not get my way. They need to hear my concerns... my superior advice... my complaints... my corrections... my rebukes. I have to keep everybody straight. If I don't act, this thing might get out of hand.

And I might not get my way.

How many decisions have you felt compelled to act on that, looking back, would have turned out so much better if you had just waited a while? How many comments have you made that were so utterly ineffective and unnecessary... and even destructive?

Our Father tells us, "Be still and know that I am God" (Psa. 46:10). I want to know God. I want to go deep with my Father. Don't you? So, I'm learning to be still and to wait. And as I do, it becomes so clear why my Father wants me to be still.

When I am still and wait on God, I always see his best. Not mine… his. When I wait on God and the guidance and power of his Spirit within me, the result is always superior to anything I could cause. Not sometimes, but always.

Waiting on the Spirit's guidance brings me closer to my Lord… every time. I get to see his movement. I get to see his power at work. None of which are possible when I am acting and reacting on my own impulse. Ignoring this spiritual rhythm of life creates complications, hurt feelings, confusion, and suffering.

Can you see it's safe to wait if you live in a God-saturated world? It's safe to wait if you see the Holy Spirit permeating your life. But if not, you must act and react quickly, and often forcefully, because it's all up to you. If you live in a "you"-saturated world, you must be assertive, demanding, and quick to act in your own self-interest. You must straighten *them* out.

Ugh. That is the essence of the C-minus life.

One last thing for those of you thinking, "Sam, you're just out of touch with reality. No one can operate in this world, running a business and a busy family, with this 'wait' approach."

But this is not about waiting on God to do something for me. Instead, it's about waiting on God to guide me. And yes, at times, waiting on the Holy Spirit to move ahead of me.

Of course, there will be times when acting quickly is necessary. At these times, we must trust God to guide us even as we act quickly. But, come on, we both know this is about five percent of the time. Our not waiting because we want to act quickly… to get our way… is the other 95 percent of the time.

Delight in him, and wait on the Holy Spirit to guide you. At times, wait for him to move and act ahead of you. Learn to be still. You'll be amazed at how your Heavenly Father works and how many problems and hurts you will avoid.

5

Narrowing Gates, Expanding Life

Jesus cautions us first to find the narrow gate that leads to life because he knows the current of this culture will sweep us right by it. After passing through that first, narrow gate to salvation, Jesus continues to invite us to look for even more gates as we progress in our spiritual journeys.

These gates are the passageways deeper into the Kingdom. But they get narrower the deeper we advance. You will have to drop... let go of... the things in your life that won't fit into the Kingdom and therefore won't fit through the narrowing gates. And the incredibly wonderful surprise is these narrowing gates lead to an ever-expanding life.

Narrower = expansive? Yes!

Okay, let's get specific.

If you want to keep advancing with Jesus toward the top, you will find it necessary to bump your trajectory from time to time because you will always plateau at some point. Let's say you're not sure you're really growing spiritually, or maybe you've just flattened out. You're frustrated (I hope) and want more. But how to get off this plateau and bump your spiritual trajectory upward?

You have two choices: new activities or a new surrender.

Just a word on activities. Taking on a more intense Bible study, digging into a challenging Christian book, attending an overnight conference, or taking on any of the spiritual disciplines such as

Scripture memorization, solitude and silence, extended prayer, or fasting... can help to bump your trajectory.

But not if you are taking on an activity just to take on an activity... just to feel better about being spiritually busy.

However, surrender will always bring us to a narrow gate, and the challenge is, "Are we willing to 'slim down', by letting go of... surrendering... whatever it is God has laid on our hearts?"

My friend Patrick and I decided to bump our workout trajectories by teaming up with Bobo for personal training. We both workout steadily but were sensing we had plateaued. We wanted things to be different, so we had to do things differently.

Bobo first designed a five-small-meals-a-day program and then started us on some rather challenging workout routines. After a couple of weeks, I had gained four pounds and expressed my frustration to Bobo.

So he asked about my personal habits, and I mentioned I might have a glass of red wine or two... two or maybe three nights a weekend. No big deal and certainly no sin.

But Bobo said, "I thought you wanted to grow. I thought you were taking this seriously. Sam, if you want things to be different, you have to do things differently."

So I went home and contemplated this simple but penetrating truth. My solution? Cut out red wine for this seven-week program.

"Yes!" I thought. "This will cut out a ton of calories along with the snacks I tend to eat with it."

I was pumped! But then, I started to think about the cost of giving up red wine for seven weeks. And I got anxious. I'm not kidding. Could I do it? Oh, sure... I guess. Did I want to do it? Uh, no.

And then the Holy Spirit showed up and pointed out that my hesitation—let's call it what it was: my fear—was because I apparently had a little emotional dependency on the wine. Maybe it had a little mastery over me?

And that's when I knew I was standing in front of a narrow gate. It was crystal clear. I knew I couldn't advance deeper into the Kingdom while carrying this mastery. I knew I had to shed this off before I could get through this very narrow gate.

I did, and the results have been amazing: more spiritual energy, clarity, and creativity!

It is always this way when we face a narrow gate and surrender and shed to get through it. God always responds with "well done, my good and faithful servant. Come on… Enjoy this greener, expansive pasture."

So what about you? Could you do it? I don't mean wine necessarily although I bet there are many of you thinking, "I could, but I don't want to." Ha!

For you, it may be a habit… It could be a bad habit, a not-so-bad habit, or even a "good" habit. One friend realized it was golf. For another, it was girls' night out. For another, it was a grudge, a refusal to forgive. It may be a relationship. It may be your stinginess with money… or a heart attitude of resentment, judgment, or superiority.

Or… gossip. Oops.

Only you know what it is for you. But you do know. And it is blocking your advance.

Whatever it is, when you hear the Holy Spirit's conviction that it needs to go, will you listen and respond? Will you face that narrow gate and surrender? Or will you hear the serpent's voice instead who is saying, "Did God really say that? Oh, come on… That wasn't God. That was just that 721 guy. He's a fanatic. No need to bother about it. You're just fine."

But you're not. And God loves you so much that he doesn't want to leave you the way you are even though he loves you perfectly either way. But it is his perfect love that invites you to go deeper.

Each gate is a matter of you giving up your claim to your right to yourself. It really is that simple.

God will not ask you to surrender what you cannot but what you will not. And it is always for your good.

No one looking back on the difficult challenge of surrendering something and advancing through the next narrowing gate will ever regret it. I thank God over and over both for pulling me through a few gates I refused to enter on my own as well as encouraging me through several more.

I hope and trust he will never stop because they always lead to greener pasture and an ever-expanding life.

Always. Every time.

Jesus is inviting you to go deeper. Will you?

6

Lighten Up & Tighten Up

After 14 weeks of seeking to understand what "keeping the Sabbath holy" means, I am still wandering around clumsily. My Sabbath-keeping is very much a work in progress. But, there is progress, and the fog is lifting. I am starting to see this gift, what an "immeasurably, abundantly more than anything we can ask for or even imagine to ask for" kind of gift this is (Eph. 3:17-19).

But so many are pushing back. A favorite refrain is, "But Jesus did away with the Old Testament Law. This is the New Testament; we live in an age of grace."

To which I might reply, "Who needs grace for a gift?"

What is your image of the OT God versus the NT Jesus? Let me guess… The OT God is angry, vengeful, and all about punishing while the NT Jesus is warm, soft, and fuzzy?

And your image of the OT laws versus this NT grace? The OT is hard, rigid, and black and white while the NT grace means, "Oh, it's alright. Just do your best, and it will be okay."

So when it comes to keeping the Sabbath holy, there is no need to get worked up about something as archaic as the Sabbath. We live in an age of grace… Right?

But this is because you are still stuck in the mindset that God is about prohibiting you, not protecting you. You still view the Sabbath commandment as a restriction, not a refuge.

So, you are still a slave to this destructive misconception. Therefore, you are missing perhaps God's greatest gift for you.

Remember that whatever is important to God is only important to him because he knows how important it is *for* you.

I would like to *command* you to spend some time with the Lord each morning, first thing, before you get your day started because I know how important it is for you. I would also like to command you to sleep eight hours, exercise regularly, and eat more protein as well as listen to more Earth, Wind & Fire. Why? Not because I get off on commanding people around but because I know how good it will be for you... especially the Earth, Wind & Fire part.

And so it is with your Heavenly Father.

The NT Jesus comes along and starts his ministry by clarifying his teaching mission:

> Do not think that I have come to abolish the Law or the Prophets; I have not come to abolish them but to fulfill them. (Matt. 5:17)

He then proceeds to *fulfill* the Sabbath commandment by knocking the props out from under the Pharisees' legalistic approach to the Sabbath. But if you think Jesus is abolishing the Sabbath... please, think again.

Jesus is saying, "Lighten up, but tighten up: Lighten up, you stiff-necked Legalists, you've lost the heart of my Father. But tighten up, you who think you can ignore my commandments. All my laws are about the heart, first, but they are still *commandments.*"

So if you still think Jesus is the warm and fuzzy God, full of grace and *only* grace, think about this...

Is it easier to not kill or to not get angry? Easier to not commit adultery or to not lust? Easier to swear an oath or "simply let your 'yes' be 'yes' and your 'no' be 'no'"? Is it easier to revenge an eye for an eye or to turn the other cheek? To love your neighbor or to love your enemy? To forgive once or to forgive over and over? (see Matt. 5-6).

Jesus' Sermon on the Mount is all about "lighten up, but tighten up, too."

When we see how Jesus plows right over our keenly crafted rationalizations and our carefully arranged loopholes, we might just long for the "rigid" OT approach. At least, then, we could ignore the spirit of the Law as long as we keep the legal part.

But Jesus tells us that "the true worshipers will worship the Father *in Spirit and in truth,* for they are the kind of worshipers the Father seeks" (John 4:23, italics added). So, no loopholes and no rationalizations.

The truth is this: "keeping the Sabbath holy" is a commandment. The spirit is this: God's Holy Spirit will show you the heart of this commandment.

When the Pharisees went nuts over Jesus' disciples picking a few pieces of grain on the Sabbath, he responded with an incredulous,

> There is far more at stake here than religion. If you had any idea what this Scripture meant—"I prefer a flexible heart to an inflexible ritual"—you wouldn't be nitpicking like this. The Son of Man is no lackey to the Sabbath; he's in charge.(Matt. 12:7, MSG)

I can hear Jesus saying, "Lighten up. It's about your heart, not a ritual, and surely not a restriction. But tighten up because I am still in charge of the Sabbath. And I am *commanding* you to "rest, relax, remember, refresh, rejuvenate, rejoice… and revere your holy Father."

Don't ignore the Sabbath; explore it. See what God has in store for you. Just try it. Start with waking up and saying, "Today is the Sabbath. It's God's day." Just start with that. And maybe, just maybe, put your to-do list aside… just for a day. Try it; it's not that scary.

Accomplish… nothing. Play and pray more.

After 14 weeks, I'm starting to feel protected from the mayhem of our push-push-push culture. This past Sunday, that urgent voice in my head kept saying, "For crying out loud, *do* something. Accomplish something!" Instead, I just read some more. I read, walked, thought, and reflected. A special day. His day. A soft, gentle day.

7

Rich Young Ruler

---

*Therefore everyone who hears these words of mine and puts
them into practice is like a wise man who built his house on
the rock... it did not fall, because it had its **foundation** on
the rock. But everyone who hears these words of mine and
does not put them into practice is like a foolish man who
built his house on sand. He lives with an uneasy anxiety because he knows his foundation is rickety.*

—Jesus in Matthew 7:24-26
(paraphrase with bold added)

If I could catch you in the midst of your busy life and ask
you a question without you having the time to think what answer
would sound the best, how would you truthfully answer this:

*What in your life, as long as it is okay, means life is okay? What is it
that, as long as it is not threatened and as long as it is there for you to rely
on, provides you with a pervasive sense that all is good? In essence, what
is the foundation upon which your happy well-being is grounded?*

To some degree, for all of us, it would be money. Please, don't
cry foul. You know it's true. But we would also have other "foun-
dations," such as success, social standing, what people think of us
and our children, our house or spouse... as well as a multitude of
other silly little gods upon which we depend.

Over time, they have become our foundation for happiness and, in an unintended reversal, have now become our masters.

We see in the Bible that the Rich Young Ruler depended on his great resume for salvation. He had it in hand and was hoping Jesus would say, "Wow, you are really something!" Instead, Jesus offered to him a defining moment, a clear-cut path into the A-plus life. His trust in his resume was blocking his salvation. Now, we see his false foundation was blocking him from experiencing the A-plus life.

It was hard for that young man to take Jesus up on his offer. He actually said no to God. Sounds crazy, doesn't it? Why would anyone say no to God? But, we do.

In order to explore why we would, let's start with what an alcoholic and a drug addict have in common. Could it be a total dependence on a substance? Okay, but let's dig deeper. What do the following also have in common: a famous person... a beautiful woman... a superstar athlete... a very successful person... a very smart intellectual... a very religious person... a socially prominent person... a very rich person.

What do all of these have in common that makes it hard for them to enter the A-plus life, including the alcoholic and addict? They have something other than Jesus Christ on which they think they can depend. And thus, their entry into the "Kingdom life that is truly life" is prevented.

We might be tempted to say these people already have the A-plus life. For this young ruler and for us, there is no greater obstacle into the A-plus life than the illusion that you already have it.

Picture any of these people standing before Jesus, like the rich young ruler, asking, "What must I do to inherit eternal life?"

Jesus would reply to them,

You don't have to wait to inherit it; the Kingdom has come, and you can step into it now. But if you want to enter, you must surrender your dependence on your money, beauty, celebrity status, success, religious formalities, prominence at church, social popularity, or whatever else you rely on... not because it is necessarily bad but because you need it too much and it's too rickety for the A-plus life.

Jesus might not insist that we rid our lives of any of these things—although that may be appropriate at times—but that we must surrender our reliance on them because entry into the Kingdom is open only to those whose reliance and trust are placed on the King.

That bears repeating… Entry into the Kingdom and then traveling deeper into the A-plus life is open only to those whose trust is in the King.

Jesus meant it when he said, "No one can serve two masters" (Matt. 6:24). It is obvious that the alcoholic's master has become alcohol. But for the rich young ruler, it is not so obvious, nor is it for us because our masters are not so ugly. But Jesus tells us as he told this young man, "You must transfer your trust from your current master to me if you want to enter life. The A-plus life is built upon the foundation of me, only."

And now, lovingly, Jesus had this young man at a crossroads of faith, a spiritual crisis, and a chance for a defining moment in his life. Would he take it? Would he step into the Kingdom and begin his journey into the A-plus life? Or, would he retreat back and continue to rely on his self-made, rickety foundation of sand?

What is it you depend on? What is your foundation for happiness? Stop now and think deeply, please. We must all transfer our trust, our dependence, from whatever and wherever else it is to Jesus.

Will you?

8

Whole House Renovation or Just Adding Religion?

As the Apostle Paul asked the new disciples he bumped into at Ephesus:

> Did you receive the Holy Spirit when you believed?
> Did you take God into your mind only, or did you also
> embrace him with your heart? Did he get inside you?
> (Acts 19:2, MSG)

Having the Holy Spirit in your mind only but not *inside* you reminds me of our advice to engaged couples. Typically, it goes like this: The young man is expecting marriage to be like adding an addition to his house. His house (his life) will be pretty much the same, he assumes… but, of course, with his new wife added.

But the young lady is expecting a whole-house renovation! She's expecting everything to change, including – and especially – her new husband.

He might be a mere spectator; she's a participant.

And being a participant is what God wants for you. Listen to Peter, a former spectator:

> …he has given us his very great and precious promises,
> so that through them you may **participate** in the divine
> nature… (2 Pet. 1:4, bold added)

What a precious promise: to actually participate—not in a religion or just in church... that's for spectators—but in the divine nature.

But it involves a whole-house renovation to which we independent humans are loathe to submit.

Me, too. I've done it the hard way: room by room, begrudging each transformation. And this kind of remodeling approach takes longer. The mess and the frustration abound, and it cost me oh so much more.

Until recently. Now, I am surrendering to and welcoming a whole-house renovation. None of this remodeling stuff for me. Total renovation. From the studs out.

Room-by-room remodeling is a herky-jerky way to live and is most unsatisfying. So if you are still missing Jesus' promise of the "life to the full," take a look at your renovation approach.

Trying to add Jesus without being filled and empowered by the Holy Spirit results in a tired, beat-up, and harried attempt at being religious.

Jesus had a message for you about this:

> Come to me, all you who are weary and burdened, and
> I will give you rest. Take my yoke upon you and learn
> from me for I am gentle and humble in heart, and you
> will find rest for your souls." (Matt. 11:28-29)

Did you receive the Holy Spirit as a whole house renovation, or just religion as an addition?

9

Not Perfect but Good Enough?

I tell you the truth, it is hard for a rich man to enter the
kingdom of heaven. Again I tell you, it is easier for a camel
to go through the eye of a needle than for a rich man to enter
the kingdom of God.

—Matthew 19:23-24

Tim Keller says, "A good way to avoid Jesus is to avoid
sin." If we are good enough, who needs a Savior? If we are good
enough, who needs all that messiness of surrender, and heart-
wrenching confession and repentance?

No sin, no need for a Savior.

But who are we kidding? We know better, deep down inside.

The Rich Young Ruler knew better, too. So he approached Jesus, asking what good things he must do to get eternal life. What he
was really asking is what *else* good must he do, because he was doing a lot of good already. When Jesus listed several of the Top 10, he
responded, "I already do all those!"

But for some reason he approached Jesus for help, in spite of
his really good goodness. Did he realize, deep down, that acting
good is not good enough? It certainly seems so.

Jesus may as well have been saying, "It is hard for a man or
woman rich…in good deeds…to enter the Kingdom." Why would

they need to surrender and be forgiven? They are already pretty darn good. Not perfect, mind you, but oh come on, way better than most.

And since God grades on the curve, I'm okay and you're okay. Or at least good enough.

We know there is no good that is good enough. But we try anyway. We are hooked on performance. When we try to act good in order to perform well, we are actually living out of fear, and our performance will grade out at a C-minus at best.

Did you good performers get that? A C-minus at best.

But when you are a born again child of the Father, pleasing him replaces performance.

Surrender is so much simpler than performance. If you surrender "my claim to my right to myself," (Oswald Chambers) your good deeds will flow naturally from love, not fear. And that is the A+ life to the full.

10

For You, With You, & Before You?

I press on to take hold of that for which Christ Jesus took hold of me.

—Philippians 3:12

I want you to know...Jesus wants you to know, God is *for* you, he is *with* you, and he is *before* you. In all things and in all ways, he is for you. He looks at you and beams, "That's my child, and I am well pleased with him...with her!" And he is always with you. He is even out before you, leading the way.

And when you "take hold of that," you will begin to see him out before you, leading the way, clearing the way, and making your paths straight (Prov. 3:5-6)...even amidst the crooked, rocky, and scary detours on which we often find ourselves.

So, given this assurance, God says through the Apostle Paul, "I want you to take hold of *that* for which my Son took hold of you." God is saying to you...to *you*...today, "I have a plan, a purpose for you, and I want you to take hold of it. I don't want you to miss out on anything I have for you." Because you are...

God's workmanship, created in Christ Jesus to do good works, which God prepared in advance for [you] to do. (Eph. 2:10)

The Greek word for "workmanship" would be better translated as "craftsmanship." Craftsmanship indicates high quality, unique quality, individualized attention, personal pride, and the "finest of wines." In God's eyes, you are designer quality. Nothing off-the-rack about you.

Following Jesus, as you learn to take hold of *that*, means you are participating relationally and personally in his individualized plan and purpose for you. It is not like wandering around in a big-box store, frustrated and desperately hoping to find an employee for some guidance and help.

Because Jesus is for you, he is with you, and he is out before you. Always.

He encourages you with this promise:

If God gives such attention to the appearance of wildflowers—most of which are never even seen— don't you think he'll attend to you, take pride in you, do his best for you? What I'm trying to do here is to get you to relax, to not be so preoccupied with getting, so you can respond to God's giving. (Matt. 6:30 MSG)

Do you truly believe God is *for* you? Come on, now...Don't give me the Sunday-school answer. You might assume he loves you because, "God so loved the world" (John 3:16).

But do you think he *likes* you? Is he your friend? He does, and he can be. Taking hold of *that* means seeing that Jesus laughs with you and smiles with you at your idiosyncrasies. He is pleased with you, even proud of you, even though you cannot possibly understand why. He says,

"That's my boy! Isn't he wonderful?" And, "Look at her. I'm so proud of her!"

That is all about feeling energy and enthusiasm from Jesus, positive reinforcement...not disapproval and condemnation.

Do you remember that poor girl caught in adultery and tossed down at Jesus' feet? Listen to his delicate response to her:

> Jesus straightened up and asked her, "Woman, where are they? Has no one condemned you?" "No one, sir," she said. "Then neither do I condemn you," Jesus declared. "Go now and leave your life of sin." (John 8:10-11)

"I want you to 'leave your life of sin' because I am with you, and I will help you to do so. But 'neither do I condemn you,'" Jesus is saying.

Jesus will not accept your sinful ways, precisely because he is so much *for* you. He knows how heavy and burdensome your sins and dysfunctions are, and he wants you to leave them behind. But this is a far cry from negative condemnation. Instead, he is calling you to follow him as he walks with you and even out before you.

May you allow Jesus to fully take hold of you, as you press on to take hold of him, living "freely and lightly, learning the unforced rhythms of his grace" (Matt. 11:28-30, MSG).

11

Surrendering Your Throne

When we live in the Kingdom of Me, perched atop our silly little thrones, strutting around like the ridiculous little royalties we think we are, the best we can hope for is a C-minus life. Often, it's closer to a D, and many times it's a flat-out failing F. The F life is obvious, and therefore may compel us to get off the Throne of Me and surrender to the true King. This is a wonderful result, to say the least.

The D life is a miserable life, but apparently not miserable enough to move some people to take action…to seek change.

But it's the C-minus life that is the most dangerous, because we are lulled into a "just mowing-the-lawn" approach to life. We just get through each day, keeping the grass cut and the lawns of our lives nice for everyone to see, but the days become weeks, months, and years that drift by.

The C-life is the most insidious, and thus to be feared the most.

But Jesus comes along and offers an invitation to a richer life, the A-plus life in the Kingdom of Him, not Me. This life is a refreshing, cleansing, freeing life of trust. Jesus offers a life of clarity, energy, and creativity that flows naturally through the Kingdom among us, powered by the Holy Spirit. But only if you want it. He won't force it on you.

Sometimes, I wish he would, don't you? "Jesus, just bind and gag me and force me into surrendering my throne. My kingdom has too much sway over me. I've been atop this throne for too long. Make me give it up, please!"

Jesus smiles lovingly and says, "If you want it, I'll take you deeper, deeper into the Promised Land. But only if." Jesus so often preceded his invitations by an 'if.' He is not going to force it on you, this A+ life to the full. You must want it.

At various times in our journey we hear Jesus' invitation to go deeper. Each time we will find ourselves at a gate, a crossroads if you will, and the question becomes, "Will I stay atop my throne and continue to try to control things, and people, my way, or will I surrender and follow Jesus…his Way?"

Stay atop your throne: Misery

Surrender your throne: Love, joy, peace, patience

It is your choice.

12

Where's Your Focus?

What really matters in this upside-down world is that we trust Jesus—we trust him for our salvation, and we trust him in the details of our day-to-day lives.

> "The only thing that counts is faith (trust), expressing itself through love." (Galatians 5:6, 'trust' added)

If you actually did act and you actually did live trusting your Heavenly Father—in the details—, would you not be more relaxed? Does this describe you? Relaxed? Living with a calm, relaxed pace? Perhaps on a really good day. Perhaps not on most days?

Now that we know what really matters to Jesus, how in this crazy culture do we maintain our trust?

Focus.

We must focus on Jesus, and his constant presence in our lives … in the details of our lives. When I read the scriptures, I see a multitude of statements such as, "and God caused," and, "God made," and, "God was with them." And my favorite: "But God."

But God.

Life is swirling out of control? But God. The contract fell through: And God. The IRS called, your child is off the rails, the doctor called, your spouse's lawyer called—and God. But God.

I have decided to live my life in an "And God, but God" world. In essence, a God-saturated world. My personal application is to choose to see Him in all my details. All of them.

Recently I was in the park with our dogs, letting them run around and have a big time. I had already used my supply of two poop bags a piece for each of them. (Who is the master and who is the servant in that picture?) As I followed Gus, I came across a discarded, unused poop bag, and my first thought was frustration at people leaving trash around.

But I decided to apply my new "And God, but God" focus, and lo and behold, a minute later Gus required another bag. I'm sure it was a mere coincidence that I had just found a bag lying around, but I made the choice—and it is a choice, isn't it?—to thank Jesus. A silly thing, I know.

Two days later I received Sports Illustrated featuring Clemson's national championship on the cover. It was to my address, but to someone who has never lived at my address. I would have wanted a copy of this issue, but would never have remembered or taken the time to go somewhere to buy one.

So I decided to apply my "And God, But God" focus, and thanked Him for this little gift. Another silly thing. Probably just another coincidence, and I understand this sounds silly and naïve to many of you, but here is my question to you:

What is the harm in this focus? The downside is I may give credit to Jesus when he wasn't actually involved. That is, if he ever isn't. Did the Savior of the world supply a poop bag and a magazine? Sounds ridiculous, I know. But the upside is my life becomes focused on Jesus, in the details, throughout the day. And therefore, I can ... relax.

That, my friend, is a huge upside.

One last thought: If I choose *not* to practice this focus on Jesus in the details, I will undoubtedly, unwittingly choose to focus on ... me. And that is a huge downside.

13

Going Deeper

It would seem that Our Lord finds our desires not too strong, but too weak. We are half-hearted creatures, fooling about with drink and sex and ambition when infinite joy is offered us, like an ignorant child who wants to go on making mud pies in a slum because he cannot imagine what is meant by the offer of a holiday at the sea. We are far too easily pleased.

—C.S. Lewis, *The Weight of Glory*

Picture with me a scene at the beach. The water is crystal clear Caribbean blue, with that wonderful wash of emerald green. There are several people in our scene:

The first person is asleep under a big umbrella.

The next is standing up throwing a Frisbee.

The next is waist deep in the water.

The next is body-surfing in the waves.

The next is out fifty feet or so swimming.

The next is out a ways in a boat.

The next is snorkeling next to the boat.

The next is scuba diving around a shallow coral reef.

And the next is scuba diving deeper around a shipwreck.

Pause please for a moment and fix this scene in your mind.

What is the person throwing the Frisbee saying to the person lying lazily under the umbrella? And what is the person standing waist deep in the water saying to the friend throwing the Frisbee?

As we skip to the person in the boat, what is he or she saying to the people on the shore? And the person snorkeling to the person in the boat? And the scuba diver to the person snorkeling?

By now you get the picture. Each is saying to the previous person something like, "Come on, throw the Frisbee with me. Come in the water, it is so nice. Come out on my boat, you won't believe how much prettier it is out here.

"Put on a mask and snorkel and come in the water with me. You can see so much more with a mask on. You must try scuba diving, you can go deeper and stay longer, and see so much more. Get down here on this wreck. The fish are amazing and I think there might be a treasure inside!"

Jesus is always calling us to go deeper in our relationship with him. He knows the riches we are missing. He knows the beauty, the unfathomable beauty, awaiting us – and the love, the joy, the peace, and the patience as our experience with him grows more intimate. He is calling you to go deeper, but he will not force you to. You must want it.

Do you?

Each person in our beach scene has seen and experienced more than the previous person. And each is saying, "There is so much more. You have to see this!"

But the previous person may likely respond, "I'm okay right here. I'm doing just fine. What's the fuss about? That will take too much effort. I'm sure that is good for you, but not for me.

Or …"You're just a fanatic."

Or … "I'm too busy right now."

Or … "I'll get to that later."

Oh my.

Where are you on this beach scene? Are you comfortable right where you are? Do you doubt there is really that much more to see? Do you view your friend who is stepping out and going deeper as perhaps just a little more, how might we say it, emotional, and even a tad too zealous?

Would you *say* you want more, but are you too busy, too distracted?

Or … are you pursuing an ever-deepening relationship with Jesus? Really pursuing? Are you digging deeper for more? Are you seeking his life to the full he promised?

I will simply say this: There is so much more. And you are missing it. Wherever you are, there is so much more to see, so much richness yet to experience.

14

Going Deeper: No Excuses

Imagine Satan meeting with three young demons as they set out on their first job assignments. He asks each what their strategy will be.

The first says, "I will tell them there is no Hell."

The second says, "I will tell them there is no Heaven."

To each Satan responds, "That won't work. Deep down inside they know better."

But the third young demon says proudly, "I'm going to tell them there is no hurry."

Satan beams and enthusiastically declares, "You will get millions that way!"

Last week we pictured a scene at the beach. People are napping, throwing the Frisbee, splashing about in the shallow water, all the way to snorkeling and even deep sea diving.

I'm sure you have experienced this yourself. I would guess at some point you have tried to convince a friend or family member to join you in the fun. You likely said something like:

"Come on, you've got to try this. You will be amazed at what you can see! You're missing it."

I am just as sure you have both heard, as well as said yourself:

"I'm okay right here. I'm doing just fine."

Or ... "I'm too busy right now." Or ... "I'll get to that later."

Now let's suppose the deep water diving is what God wants for you. It is, you should know. But you don't really care. You're busy. You're distracted by too many ... not even close to truly important ... activities.

You would *say* you care, you would even *declare* that you care, but come on, "If it's important to you, you will make it happen. If it's not, you will make excuses."

Jesus told a story about a man who wanted to throw a huge, over-the-top banquet, replete with the finest of foods and drink. A gala not to be equaled, and surely not to be missed.

> "A certain man was preparing a great banquet and invited many guests. At the time of the banquet he sent his servant to tell those who had been invited, 'Come, for everything is now ready.'" (Luke 14:16)

Sounds a bit like our beach scene, doesn't it?

But listen to what Jesus says next: "But they all alike began to make excuses" ... all in essence saying, "I'll get to that later."

God's blunt response to their excuses may surprise you: "I tell you, not one of those who were invited will get a taste of my banquet."

Jesus is telling us, he is telling you, that his Father doesn't appreciate you taking his invitation lightly. He is not interested in your excuses. Even more, he is angered by your lack of interest ... by your lukewarm attitude.

Yes, angered. (That may sting a bit, and if it does, let it.)

Jesus is calling you to a deeper relationship. He wants you to know him. He wants you to know his Father. The deeper you go, the more his world and his kingdom will open up to you.

I close with God's own invitation to you:

> I keep asking that the God of our Lord Jesus Christ, the glorious Father, may give you Holy Spirit energy and clarity, so that you may know him better. ... so that you may know the riches of his glorious inheritance for those who dig deeper, and his incomparably great power for those who surrender their lives to him. (Ephesians 1:17-19, Sam's paraphrase)

15

Life to the Full: The Submit Game

Jesus stated plainly his mission was to show to us and deliver to us a new Life:

> "I have come so that they may have life, and have it to the full." (John 10:10)

Let's pause and ask ourselves, "What would this Life to the Full look like in our relationships ... in the day to day details and interactions?

For an abbreviated answer let's start with the basics:

Priorities – Relationships

As Jesus fills us with his Full Life, we see the world around us with a new perspective. The fog of the culture of this world is burned off by his Light, and our blurred vision begins to focus on what is truly important in life.

We may say this happens naturally as one gets older, and, yes, this is true. For the most part. But remember, I deal on a daily basis with real people, and I continue to see a culture-induced-cataract in many "grown-ups."

Too many people are still prisoners of Jesus' third soil type in his Parable of the Four Soils:

"... they are choked by life's worries, riches and pleasures, and they do not mature." (Luke 8:14)

These folks' perspective and priority is skewed, and they miss what is most important:

Relationships

I have found one solution to all our relationship problems, issues and challenges: Die to Self. I am often tempted to interrupt men as we talk about their marriage problems and say, "Try dying to Self for a month or two and then come back and let's talk about your issues."

I believe most of their issues will dissipate with this practice, don't you? The Holy Spirit crystallizes this idea of dying to Self, especially in marriage, as he states through Paul:

> Submit to one another out of reverence for Christ. (Ephesians 5:21)

Submit to one another. Let the other person have it their way. Not because the other deserves this, and certainly not because they are above you. But because your perspective has shifted, and you now see that so many times you just wanted to do it your way. You wanted to get your way.

Can I get an "Amen?"

Imagine this marriage conversation:

> Wife: "Honey, I was thinking we could stop by the store on the way to the game and look for those pots I have been wanting to find."
> Husband: (First to himself): "That makes no sense. It is not on the way. We could have done this any other time. There is nothing efficient about that!"

But because his perspective has shifted, he instead rethinks and says to himself: "She wants to do this. It is important to her. So what if we drive a little out of the way? So what if we miss doing such and such or seeing so and so? It makes her happy. That is all that really matters. And … it honors my Lord Jesus."

"Sweetheart, (with a sincere smile) that sounds like a perfect idea!"

Or

Husband: "Sweetheart, I want to order chicken wings and watch The Outlaw Josey Wales movie tonight."

Wife: (First to herself): "Chicken wings? Ugh. And he'll get extra Ranch dip too! And that Western again? We've watched it a hundred times already."

But instead she says to herself: "It makes him happy. We will be sitting together. I can nibble around the edges and there are a few interesting parts in the movie. And besides, he just loves this."

"Honey, (with a sincere smile) that sounds great!"

Really, would it kill you to practice letting him or her have their way more often? Imagine a couple who so embraced this approach they almost made a game out of submitting to one another – out of reverence for Jesus.

Now for those of you who are sneering and asking, "But what about if my wife or my husband is wrong, and it will lead to a bad thing, even a catastrophe?" You're just dodging and you know it. How often does that scenario come up, versus the myriad of times it truly does not matter one bit if we do it their way?

So I say, shift your perspective to what is truly important: relationships. Healthy, positive, thriving, joyful and fulfilling relationships. And practice, make a game out of it, letting your spouse do it their way.

Life to the full!

16

Who is in Control?

In our opening meetings with the men at 721 we put up on the whiteboard the different emotions and feelings we are experiencing during this crazy time of politics and pandemics, shutdowns, riots, violence, jobs obliterated, no school, and even an asteroid heading our way.

I think it would be helpful for you to do the same. I have learned over the years that if we will write down our fears, worries and anxieties, they often lose their hold over us. Yes, just writing them down helps! Many years ago, when I was in a deep ditch, and had not yet learned that feelings are such disastrous masters, I was overwhelmed constantly by my feelings of fear, anxiety, even dread and hopelessness.

I decided to write down the worst things that could happen, and then I put them in a shoebox. A year later I pulled them out and lo and behold, only one of my worst-case scenarios actually happened. The others never materialized. The one that did happen was nowhere near as bad as I had feared. And of course Jesus worked wonderfully good things out of that bad.

So ... a lot of worrying and stressing for nothing.

What words would you put on the whiteboard to express your feelings today during this most uncertain time?

Fear – Anger – Future – Uncertainty – Our Country – Frustrated – Payback – Punish – Enemies – Revenge – Lawlessness – Baffled – Confused – Hopeless?

What questions might you add to this list?

Why does God allow this?

Does he care about our country?

Is he involved in the details?

Does he even care about the details?

Does he care about my personal details?

And most pertinent: Who is in Control?

To frame our perspective on these, allow me to ask a few questions for you to ponder.

Is the USA eternal?

Are the Democrats and the Republicans eternal?

Is China eternal?

Is this pandemic eternal?

Is the media – the stock market – the upcoming election – Trump Biden – Antifa – riots – economic collapse … eternal?

But most pertinent: Are you?

The answers: All no's and the last a big yes.

Which leads us to pull back and examine the macro and the micro of our current state of the union. That would be the macro state of our USA union, and much more important the micro state of your union with Jesus.

The Macro: If you asked me if God cares about the state of our Union, the USA, I would answer, "Yes, I feel sure he does. But I do not know the how, what, why, when, where of his caring."

The Micro: But here is what I know beyond any doubt: He cares immensely about the state of your union with him. Because he cares immensely about the state of your soul.

I am certain God did not allow this C-19 virus just to boost Sam's spiritual journey. I am equally certain he is not allowing this chaos in our country just to boost Sam's spiritual journey.

But I am 100% certain he wants to use these experiences to bring me closer to him. And he wants me … and you … to be a part of this closing-the-gap process.

The macro issues and the resulting questions all pale in comparison to the micro issues in your heart and your soul. He wants to use every experience to bring us closer to him. And why? Because he loves you, and yes, he cares about your details.

He knows the closer you are to him, the richer your life will be. He wants the A+ Life to the Full for you, and the only way to find this life – the only way, my friend – is to close any gap between you and Jesus.

The essential Micro question for you is: How do I use this crazy uncertainty to get closer to Jesus?

17

Facts, Faith, Feelings

We are in a mess in this country, aren't we? Chaos is all around us. Politics and pandemics, riots and ridiculous talking heads, economic disasters, jobs lost, livelihoods destroyed. If I could sit down with Jesus, here are some of the questions I would ask:

Why does God allow this?

Is he involved in the details?

Does he care about our country?

Does he care about my personal details in my day to day life?

Everything around us screams out, "No, he must not." We see the chaos and our feelings overwhelm us. Why, what, how, when? What if? How will I?

Or to be more specific:

What will happen to this country if my candidate does not win?

How will I cope with the impending disaster if the other man wins?

Who will be in control of this country?

Who will be in control of my life?

I am asking these very same questions – and often with agitation and frustration. Can you feel the anxiety? Can you feel my faith wobbling? But are there any facts I can hold onto to calm my fears and stabilize my wobbling faith?

Remember, for a follower of Jesus, the order of priority for "Feelings – Faith – Facts" is: Facts first, faith second, and feelings a distant third. Feelings are okay as servants, but disastrous masters. When my feelings take over, my faith wobbles, and fear and anxiety rule me. But if I focus on the facts, then these truths dominate my feelings, and stabilize my wobbling faith.

Anxiety and fear are then mastered by peace and joy.

So let's revisit the facts:

God is aware of and he is involved in the details of your life: Matthew 10:29-31

God loves you perfectly: 1 John 4:16-18

God is perfectly powerful: I do not believe quoting scripture here is helpful. You either accept this as a fact or not.

God is perfectly in control: If the above is a fact, then so too is this.

Dwell on these facts until they are anchored in your heart. Be sure to lock onto the perfect love of Jesus, because when his perfect love becomes a fact in your life, there will simply be no room for fear.

As the Holy Spirit says through John:"There is no fear in love. But perfect love drives out fear..." (1 John 4:18)

So as I lock onto this perfect love, any fear that tries to infiltrate and lodge in my heart is driven out, because it simply cannot find any room – it is crowded out by Jesus' perfect love.

What a way to live!

I finish with this prayer for you:

> And I pray that you, being rooted and established in love, may have power, together with all the Lord's saints, to grasp ... **the facts:** how wide and long and high and deep is the **perfect** love of Christ, and to know this **perfect** love that surpasses knowledge—that you may be filled to the measure of all the fullness of God. (Eph. 3:17-19, bold words added)

18

What is that in You?

Amidst all the chaos in our country, the message to each
of us from Jesus is, "What is that to you? You follow me." Lately I
find myself becoming distracted by questions such as, "How can
this be happening in a civilized country?" or "What is going to become of our country?" or "In what kind of country will my children
and grandchildren grow up?"

But Jesus offers a simple answer: "Sam, you follow me."

There are three Biblical examples of this simple and succinct
message that we will explore over the next three weeks. All three
bring our focus back to ourselves – to you and to me. Not others,
not the events taking place around you – you. Because you, and
your inward workings with Jesus, are all that is eternal in all this.

Today we will examine the first example.

In John 21 we find Jesus meeting several of the disciples on the
beach for breakfast. This is post-resurrection, so every encounter
with Jesus is loaded with meaning. After breakfast Jesus takes a
walk with Peter down the beach. He asks Peter three times, "Do you
love me?" After Peter answers, Jesus tells him each time, "Feed my
sheep."

Jesus is driving home to Peter that his mission, for the rest of
his life, is to take care of Jesus' followers. Jesus tells him this three
times so there can be no confusion in Peter's mind, and certainly no
distractions from his central mission.

It is as if Jesus is saying, "Peter, I know you bounce around a
lot, and are easily distracted, so I want to be absolutely clear: Your

mission in life, above all else, is to take care of my burgeoning family of followers. Is that clear, Peter? Are you picking up what I am laying down, Peter?"

One would assume Jesus has Peter's rapt attention. But … Peter is aware that John is following them, so here is what happens next:

When Peter saw him, he asked, "Lord, what about him?"

> Jesus answered, "If I want him to remain alive until I return, **what is that to you? You must follow me.**" (John 21:20-22, bold added)

I can only imagine the incredulous look on Jesus' face when he said, "What is that to you? You must follow me."

Could Peter not keep his focus for one minute? He is walking one on one with the Savior of the world. He is walking with his dear friend whom he has seen dead and now alive, and he cannot help but ask questions about other people! Of course, he is not that different from you and me. We are so easily distracted. We so easily lose focus on what really matters, and get sidetracked over other people, other events, and other issues.

News, weather and sports effectively crowd out Jesus and cloud up our perspective.

I am going to make a broad, sweeping declaration: If we focused on Jesus' response to Peter whenever we are becoming distracted or discouraged, our lives would be filled with a "light and life-giving clarity." When I am surrounded by confusion, or distractions, or whatever thoughts or whoever people are swirling around in my head, if I will just return to Jesus, the way becomes clearer.

I am sure for some of you there is real chaos in your personal lives, as well as the chaos in this country. I know it is very real and very scary for you. I know Jesus cares, and he will listen to all your concerns and worries as long as you want to talk to him about them. He will do so with sincerity and compassion. And yet, with all appropriate sensitivity, I think he would eventually smile lovingly and still say,

"What is that to you? You follow me."

Jesus is saying to me and to you:

1. "You do not need to worry about all this chaos – Keep your focus on me."

2. "When your faith wobbles because your feelings are taking over, just remember, 'You keep your eyes on me.'"

3. "And when you are so sure that whatever is troubling you is about someone else's actions or behavior, just remember, it is not about them, it is about you: What is that to you? You follow me.'"

19

Who Do You Say I am?

Amidst all the chaos in our country, the simple and suc-cinct message from Jesus to each of us is, "What is that to you? You follow me."

We must be aware of Satan's strategy: "The 3 D's: Destroy – Distract – Discourage."[i] If he can distract you and discourage you so that you miss Jesus and the eternal life he offers, he will have destroyed your soul, and that is his #1 objective. But if he loses that battle, and you do surrender your life to Jesus, then he will seek to destroy the A+ Life to the Full Jesus wants for you. He will do this by distracting and discouraging you, each day, every day.

This chaos in our country is the perfect scenario for him to advance his 3-D's strategy against you.

But Jesus offers simpler answers:

1. "What is that to you? You must follow me."
2. "Who do you say I am?"
3. "You are the man!"

Last week we explored the first of these. Today we will look at, "Who do you say I am?"

> When Jesus came to the region of Caesarea Philippi, he asked his disciples, "Who do people say the Son of Man is?"

They replied, "Some say John the Baptist; others say Elijah; and still others, Jeremiah or one of the prophets."

"But what about you?" he asked. **"Who do you say I am?"** (Matt. 16:13-15, bold added)

Let us suppose Jesus asked you, "Who do you say I am?" How would you answer him? Think about that for a moment.

Perhaps you would say, "You are God's Son." Or "You are God, because 'You and the Father are one.'" To really put the icing on the cake would be to say this, and then add, "But you are also my personal Savior – and my best friend."

If the God part is true – and it is – and if the "Personal Savior" part is true – and only you can know that – what does this mean to you? This is why, "Who do you say I am?" is such an important question. If he is God, and the Son of God, then he is:

1. Perfectly powerful
2. Perfectly in control
3. Loves you … perfectly

If "You are my personal Savior" is true, then he is:

1. Perfectly present in our life
2. Perfectly aware of your circumstances
3. Perfectly working out his plan for you in the details of your life

If all these are true, then as Jesus asked so often, "Why are you still so afraid?" If all these are true, then you can now step back amid the chaos in your life, and ask yourself the question, "Sam, who do you say Jesus is?" The answer can then bring instant clarity, and the chaos can be mitigated down to calm, confident comfort.

From chaos to calm, to confident, to comfort. I will take that over worry and anxiety, won't you?

A.W. Tozer observed, "The most important thing about you is what comes to your mind when you think of God." His is a poignant point, and if 1- 6 above come to mind when you think of God, my friend, you will have the calm, confident, comfort A+ Life.

Jesus wanted his disciples to think deeply about who he is. He wants you to do the same. The Life that is truly life hangs in the balance. At Caesarea Philippi Peter got the answer right: "You are the Messiah, the Son of the living God." (Matthew 16:16)

And that is all that truly matters.

20

You are the Man!

King David has just committed adultery with Bathsheba, and then had her husband set up to be killed in battle. The prophet Nathan is sent by God to confront the king. Nathan tells David a story about a powerful man taking terrible advantage of a simple, ordinary man, and David is incensed. He stands up and begins to condemn whoever this awful man is, but before David can even finish a sentence Nathan wheels around on him and declares, **"You are the man!"** (2 Samuel 12:7, bold added)

Oh my.

Have you ever heard or felt that clear, concise, laser conviction from the Lord?

I am likely alone in this, but I am very talented at finding the fault in other people. I am not just a star in this dismal game, I may be a superstar. Argh! But it is true. My first instinct in any negative situation is to identify what the other person has done wrong.

I wish I could say that even while I am focusing on the other person's faults, I hear the Holy Spirit saying, "What about you, Sam?" But sadly, I may be so good at finding fault in others I am temporarily blinded to any fault whatsoever of my own. Here is a typical conversation in my head:

"They are to blame. I am innocent. They are wrong. I am right. The only reason I may have any fault in this at all is because their bad behavior made me act poorly."

Now, I wish you had some experience in this so you could relate to what I am saying. But perhaps you know someone who does, and you can send this to them. I am sure they need it more than you!

Alcoholics Anonymous has a wonderful saying: "If you have a problem, you are the problem."

Think about that for a moment. How often has a situation become a problem because you made it one? Oh sure, "they" may have acted in an untoward manner. But you had a choice in that moment, didn't you? You could react, which typically means you over-react, which typically leads to a problem. This is precisely what God was doing with David. He drew him into a reaction, so he could show him he was the true problem.

Or you could respond to the situation in a measured way, thus avoiding elevating it into a problem. The other person's behavior may truly be a problem, but you become the problem when you make it about you.

We have a saying at 721 Ministries: "Trouble becomes conflict when I make it about me."

And we have a not so fun exercise at 721: We give each man a small mirror and ask him to carry it around with him – so he can hold it up to see who the problem is in any situation. Some of the men have carried the mirror around for years. They are typically the ones who cause the least problems in their families. When they are tempted to react with blame towards the other person, they remember the mirror, and God's words to David: "You are the man!"

There is so much to say about this, but I will close with this. When you are so sure you are right, and the other person is wrong – even if they are indeed wrong – challenge yourself with these ascending mirrors of self-evaluation:

1. I might not be completely right about this.
2. They might not be completely wrong.
3. I may not be right at all.

And the ultimate question:

4. Does it even matter?

If you want a little more:

I would encourage you to give Jesus your list of the people, or the person who is the problem in your life. Tell him, "If only they would _____ ," and you fill in the blank.

Lay it all out for him. All the pertinent facts, the evidence file of what they have done and what kind of a person they are.

He will listen intently. That is what he does so well. Then, after a while, Jesus just might smile and say, "You are the man! You are the woman!"

21

Two Garden Battles: Self

Easter is all about self. Actually, the entire Biblical story
is about self: the battle of our self against God.

Oh, you may think it is about the battle between Satan and God,
but Satan long ago realized his best strategy was to appeal to our
self, our control center. If he gets a foothold there, your self will ultimately dominate you, and from there Satan is on cruise control.

All sins emanate from self. This is why Jesus said, "Whoever
wants to be my disciple must deny themselves … their selfs … and
take up their cross and follow me" (Matt. 16:24).

Notice he did not say "must deny themselves *things*." We can
deny ourselves things all day long with no heart transformation.
Things are not the problem. Self is the problem.

Jesus goes on to observe, "For whoever wants to save their life
will lose it, but whoever loses their life for me will find it." Allow
me to substitute self in this passage: "For whoever wants to save
their *self* will lose it, but whoever loses their *self* for me will find the
A+ Life to the Full."

In the first Garden Satan did not have a vast array of *things* with
which to tempt Adam and Eve.

In the first Garden he only had their self to use against them.
But that was all he needed. Satan appealed to Adam and Eve's self,
and he won.

Even today, with Satan's entire arsenal at his fingertips: our
sick, and getting sicker by the day culture, and all that goes with it—

at its core, the temptation is still and always about self. Nothing has changed; the battle is always against self.

Jesus went into the Garden of Gethsemane to do battle with his self. Remember, three years prior Satan had tried to tempt Jesus in the wilderness with three appeals to his self. Afterward, "When the devil had finished all this tempting, he left Jesus until an opportune time." (Luke 4:1-13)

The Garden Battle in Gethsemane was that "opportune time."

Jesus had to do battle with his self in that garden. And Jesus won. He defeated self once and for all, so you and I could be freed from the tyranny of self.

Yes, you can be free from your self, your old self, your dominating, "What about me? What about my feelings? What's in it for me?" self. But not by yourself. You need more than self-help. You need more than a helping hand.

Jesus' Garden Battle caused him to sweat blood. Do you think you can do it on your own? You need a Savior. And you need his power to defeat your self.

From the Garden through the Cross, Jesus destroyed the work of Satan. Satan thought he was engineering the crucifixion of Jesus. He was a fool. He accidently engineered the crucifixion of self.

Now it is up to you. Will you fight the Battle of Self in your own Garden of Gethsemane? Will you?

You will need help. Each day. You will need the power of the Holy Spirit. Each day. The Cross opened this Holy Spirit power to you. Jesus made it available to you. He died for you to have this power.

Use it!

22

Would You Dip Seven Times?

Hi my name is Naaman. You probably don't know me but you can read my story in 2 Kings Chapter 5. And you should read it because it's the story of a very prideful man (is there any other kind?) who had to be humbled in order to see God for who He is. Before the events of this story unfolded, I couldn't see God, because all I could see was … me.

I learned that day that until I can see me for who I am –a man in desperate need of a Savior – I would never see God for who He is: The true King.

I was very successful: a warrior general and right-hand man to the king of Aram. Everybody loved and respected me because of all I had accomplished. And this is where I based my security: I was large and in charge, sitting high atop the throne of my life. I was in control of everything and everyone around me – or so I thought.

But you see I had this skin issue. Okay, it was leprosy, but I had hidden it from everyone because, well, it should be obvious why: Someone like me doesn't show weakness – ever. But as it got worse my Hebrew servant girl told me about this famous prophet in Israel who could cure me. I was doubtful, but I couldn't control this skin problem, and I had always been in control, so I set out for Israel.

I arrived in style at the pitiful hovel of a house in which this little prophet Elisha lived. I might have had to humble myself to even go see him, but you better believe I arrived in style. Chariots, horsemen, silver and gold. I would pay this little prophet well for his service.

I don't accept free help from anyone, don't you see? Grace is for weaklings. I have earned my way all my life. But, now get this, that little pipsqueak prophet didn't even come out to bow down to me ... uh, I mean greet me. He sent a servant out to tell me – that's right – tell *me* to go dip in the Jordan River ... seven times!

This flew all over me and I turned and left in a rage. I growled to my servant, "I thought that he would surely come out to me and stand and call on the name of the LORD his God, wave his hand[13] over the spot and cure me of my leprosy."

I wanted a ceremony. I wanted to be treated with the respect I deserve. The respect I have earned. After grumbling and throwing my little tantrum, my chief servant pointed out my true stumbling block: "My father, if the prophet had told you to do some great thing, would you not have done it?"

There it was: my pride. I couldn't see God because all I could see was me. My security was in my status, my accomplishments. Maybe yours is, too. Or maybe your security is in some thing or someone else. The details matter little; as long as you find your security in anything other than God, you will have no true security at all. None.

There is no true security in anyone or anything other than God, as your Heavenly Father.

I had to humble myself, yield to this little prophet, and dip seven times. With each return into those muddy waters: one, two, three, four ... seven ... inglorious times, grace was growing and my insecure security was flowing away with the river.

My pride had to surrender to God's grace. I couldn't earn this one. And my security had to be transferred from me to Him. Are you clinging to some false god for your security? Perhaps if you examined your life you'd see your security is based on your accomplishments, or your job, or someone you love. Or even their accomplishments?

Will you humble yourself, surrender and dip seven times to be free? Will you surrender and dip seven times to find the only true security there is?

Part 2

Gratitude

23

Grateful

We are now in the holiday season. Last week I resisted sending a Thanksgiving PG about, "What I am thankful for." I appreciate that sentiment, but I want to dig a little deeper – and perhaps push you a tad more.

I have found that a heart of gratitude is a heart of joy. Show me someone who is grateful, and I will show you someone who is full of positive energy. Jesus weighs in on this gratitude thing, too. One day he comes upon ten lepers. They cry out to him and he heals them all. But only one comes back to thank Jesus. Here is his response:

Jesus asked, "Were not all ten cleansed? Where are the other nine? Has no one returned to give praise to God except this foreigner?" Then he said to him, "Rise and go; your faith has made you well." (Luke 17:17-19)

Jesus seems indignant, doesn't he? He notices the others' lack of gratitude. Clearly, gratitude is important to Jesus.

Thus, I would hope it would be to you.

But as I said earlier, I want to dig a little deeper. I want you to learn to practice gratitude. I want you to learn to be specific about that for which you are grateful. Here are the questions I propose for you to ponder:

What has Jesus done for you?

What has he saved you from?

What have you been freed from?

What has he changed in you?

How has he opened your eyes so that you now see things differently?

Yes, these are similar, but I am trying to help you get your arms around this exercise. I want you to write down – yes, actually write down – your answers. And I want you to be specific. Think in terms of: Inside you, in relationships, and even in business. Write down specific answers that arise from the details of your life with Jesus. Nothing vague.

Therein is the catch. Can you be specific? Do you have an abundance of stories and experiences? Or are you fumbling around trying to come up with what might sound like good answers, but do not truly represent your relationship with Jesus?

One of our 721 men said this: "Sam, I was thinking about these questions, and it occurred to me that ten years ago, when I was still just a good Churchian, but did not know, yet, that I did not know Jesus, I would have tried to figure out what answers you were looking for. Like being back in college trying to answer essay questions. The truth is, ten years ago I wouldn't have had any specific answers. But now I do."

Do you agree that the more specific your answers, the deeper your relationship with Jesus? The more specific your answers, the more you are bringing him into the details of your life? And the more vague, and the harder you have to try, the more shallow?

Perhaps you may want to dig a little deeper … to bring Jesus more into the details of your life?

So I encourage you, I challenge you, I will browbeat you if necessary—*because I know how beneficial this will be*—to ponder these questions and write down your answers. And may your joy and confidence in the Lord fill you to the measure of all the fullness of God.

24

The Luckiest on the Planet

Barnabas was the apostle Paul's companion on their first missionary trip, and a giant in the growing family of Jesus followers in the new Way. Here is how he is described:

> Barnabas was a good man, full of the Holy Spirit and faith, and a great number of people were brought to the Lord. (Acts 11:24)

And do you know what his name means? "Encourager."

I am confident Barnabas was a man full of gratitude. I can just picture him at the gatherings, walking among the Believers, spending time with individuals and families, constantly encouraging them, lifting them up, digging deep into their needs, showing compassion, and strengthening the new Believers.

Could he be anything other than a man full of joy and gratitude?

I do not know much more about him, but I do not need more information. A man like that, described as we see above, is a man whose heart is overflowing with positive energy and thankfulness.

I want to be like that. I want to be described that way. Don't you?

So, I must practice gratitude. Yes, practice, because this world—and Satan—will constantly distract and discourage me. I will lose my focus and start feeling sorry for myself. Or worse, start to criticize and complain. And when I am criticizing and complaining, it is a sure bet I have lost my focus on just how blessed I am.

So I must learn to focus on gratitude.

I do this by writing down all my many blessings. I think about the various aspects of my life, and how lucky I am, and *I write them down*. I have index cards and post-it notes all over the place, where, instead of doodling, or dawdling, I write down the gifts and graces Jesus has lavished on me.

This is a practice that now comes naturally to me, because, even though I have so much farther to go, I am already overflowing with gratitude.

And when I am stressed, or my faith is wobbling a bit, or my perspective is becoming cloudy and somewhat myopic, if I stop and remember all my many blessings—yes, how lucky I am—my stress level dissipates, my faith strengthens, and my perspective shifts from negative to positive. You see, when I remember what he has already done for me, and in me, I can see more clearly what he is doing now, in the present details of my life.

I do not have to ask, "Where are you? Will you come through this time? Are you paying attention to this, Jesus?" Because I already have all the evidence I need. My specific answers give me specific faith, and my wobbly feelings are pushed to the rear, where they belong.

Feelings are okay as servants, but disastrous masters.

That is why writing down your specific blessings is so helpful. As I practice focusing on all the major and minor miracles in my life, and contemplate all Jesus has done in me, and for me, and with me, I can look at most any situation and say, "Thank you now, Jesus, before I see how you work this out, because, based on all the *obvious* evidence, I know I will be thanking you later."

25

Water to Wine: Ordinary to Spectacular

When you think of God what words come to mind? Are they positive, negative or just kind of flat? Beyond my childhood years, beginning with my idiot teenage years and extending until I actually met Jesus, my descriptive words would have ranged from negative to flat. Words like pedantic and petty, or boring, judgmental, and confining and condemning.

To me he was a "bread and water God." Words such as fun and feasting, lavish, generous, happy and celebrating would have been foreign to me. I would have said his purpose was to run a tight ship, without a lot of fun being had, and his passion was, well, only aroused when he became angry.

I was so wrong.

Jesus makes two statements that define his purpose and his passion much more accurately than my dimwit ideas:

> And no one pours new wine into old wineskins. Otherwise, the wine will burst the skins, and both the wine and the wineskins will be ruined. No, they pour new wine into new wineskins. (Mark 2:22)

> Do not think that I have come to abolish the Law or the Prophets; I have not come to abolish them but to fulfill them. (Matt. 5:17)

Jesus is first saying he is bringing new wine, a new way of doing things. But he is also saying he is not doing away with the old wine, the old way of doing things. But instead—and do not miss this—he is *fulfilling* God's original purpose and passion. He is fulfilling the Old Testament ways, as in filling-to-the-full, even to overflowing.

He is going to live out in full Technicolor the purpose of all those Old Testament laws.

And because he is Jesus, and typically gives us real-life demonstrations just in case we are too myopic to understand his meaning, his first miracle is to change ordinary water into spectacular wine. Ordinary to spectacular.

No, he is no bread and water God. He is a God of feasts, celebrations, and lavish love. And he always has been. That crusty Old Testament prophet Isaiah recorded God's own words about his purpose and passion:

> On this mountain the Lord Almighty will prepare a
> feast of rich food for all peoples, a banquet of aged wine
> — the best of meats and the finest of wines. (Isa. 25:6)

You gotta love that, don't you?

In John 2 we see Jesus at a wedding banquet … having fun. But the wine has run out and his mother Mary comes to him with the problem. Jesus responds by taking six big jars of ordinary water and turning them into—are you ready?—eight hundred bottles of the finest wine. Eight hundred bottles. Of "a banquet of aged wines — the finest of wines."

This is no bread and water Jesus we serve.

Now to be sure there are times when bread and water are just the right thing for me. Jesus knows when I need just that, and so for a season my "feasts" may consist of bread and water. But later, when I have grown spiritually, and closer to Jesus, precisely because of that season of bread and water, I have always—always—looked back and realized that season, too, was a lavish feast of love. One that I needed so desperately, but just did not know it.

Next week we will dive more deeply into Jesus' "first sign" of water to wine. But for now I want to ask you to think about two things:

1. Where is your wine running out?

2. Where do you doubt ... cannot seem to trust or believe ... perhaps have lost hope ... that Jesus will show up to produce eight hundred bottles of the finest wine out of the ordinary water in your life?

26

Who He is—What He Cares About

Jesus is at a wedding, having fun, when his mother Mary comes to him with a dilemma.

> When the wine was gone, Jesus' mother said to him, "They have no more wine." John 2:3

What Jesus does next tells us a lot about himself:

> Nearby stood six stone water jars, the kind used by the Jews for ceremonial washing, each holding from twenty to thirty gallons.
> Jesus said to the servants, "Fill the jars with water"; so they filled them to the brim. Then he told them, "Now draw some out and take it to the master of the banquet." They did so, and the master of the banquet tasted the water that had been turned into wine.
> Then he called the bridegroom aside and said, "Everyone brings out the choice wine first and then the cheaper wine after the guests have had too much to drink; but you have saved the best till now." (John 2:6-10)

Jesus answers a need with eight hundred bottles of choice wine. Is this perhaps a tad over the top? Perhaps. But it is not unusual for Jesus. Just for the fun of it I like to think of Jesus performing this miracle, and then looking at his disciples with a wink and a nod and saying, "Now that's how I roll."

My dear friend Doug Greenwold of Preserving Bible Times taught me to ask three questions as I studied Biblical stories. "What does this passage tell us about:"

1. Who God is
2. What he cares about
3. How he does things

Who Jesus is (Is who God is)

Social and Relational

He is at a wedding with his family and his pals. Stop and think about that for a moment. The Savior of the world, God Almighty, creator of the universe, is taking the time to ... socialize.

He is at a minimum a fun guy. His enemies accused him of being a drunk and a glutton. (Matthew 11:19) He was neither, of course. But if they are accusing him of this then he is obviously a fun person to be around.

One of my favorite images is God walking in the cool of the evening as he hung out with Adam and Eve. (Genesis 3:8) Isn't that a wonderful picture of a relational God?

Who Jesus Is & What He Cares About

Caring and Compassionate

(Compassionate: 'Com' means 'With' and 'Compassionate' means 'Suffering.')

Jesus cares enough about this young married couple to be with them in their impending social suffering and humiliation. In this culture of social reciprocity and extreme hospitality, running out of wine would have brought shame to this young couple for years.

Jesus steps in and takes care of their problem by turning an ordinary party into a spectacular feast!

Interested and involved in the details

This is perhaps the most comforting and endearing aspect to this great Jesus. Oh sure, I believe God Almighty can take care of the world, but is he interested, and will he get involved in the details of my life? In the details of my daughter's wedding?

Yes and yes and absolutely he will.

27

Water to Wine: How Jesus Does Things

Now to him who is able to do immeasurably more than all we ask or imagine.

—Eph. 3:20

Jesus is at a wedding, having fun, when his mother Mary tells him the wine is out.

Jesus answers a need with eight hundred bottles of choice wine. Eight Hundred! Is this perhaps a tad over the top? Perhaps. But it is not unusual for Jesus. After all, when he takes a few fish and a little bread and feeds five thousand men, plus their families, he still has twelve baskets overflowing with extra bread.

> They all ate and were satisfied, and the disciples picked up twelve basketfuls of broken pieces that were left over. (Luke 9:17)

When he decided to get Peter's attention he almost sunk two boats with so many fish:

> When he had finished speaking, he said to Simon, "Put out into deep water, and let down the nets for a catch."

... When they had done so, they caught such a large number of fish that their nets began to break. So they signaled their partners in the other boat to come and help them, and they came and filled both boats so full that they began to sink. (Luke 5:4,6-7)

How Jesus Does Things

Let's think for a moment about the choices Jesus had in this whole wedding affair.

1. He could have not gone at all. He is after all the long awaited Messiah. He has much to do to kick off his ministry. But Jesus is a relational God.

2. He could have said no to Mary.

Please do not miss this: Jesus never says no, as in "No, I won't respond at all to your need."

He may say, "No, I won't answer your specific request—because it would not be the best path for you," but he always responds, and always in the best way possible.

Now, as to how he could have responded with respect to the Quantity & Quality of wine:

3. He could have produced just barely enough wine, and ordinary wine at that. This would have saved the young bride and groom. And yet they would still worry about running out, again.

4. He could have produced more than enough wine, and perhaps this time a better quality, yet still just an above average wine.

5. But remember, Jesus is no bread and water God. He responds with an Ephesians 3:20, "immeasurably more than all we ask or imagine," wine.

And he will with you, too. To be sure my Ephesians 3:20 answer will look different from yours, but it will be just right for me, and just right for you. Yes, his way and his timing may try our patience. But Jesus always responds with immeasurably more than all we ask, or even imagine to ask, and always in just the perfect, customized response to your need and to mine.

That is how Jesus does things.

But my question to you is this:

When you approach Jesus with your prayers, and your needs, which of the above 1. – 5. responses do you expect? Do you think he won't even show up, or will say no, or will at best respond with just barely enough, and ordinary at that?

My friend, may you learn that Jesus always responds with immeasurably more than all we ask, or even imagine to ask, and may the eyes of your heart be enlightened so you may see his response for the Ephesians 3:20 gift it always is.

28

The New Life

The angel vanished as quickly as he had appeared. We found ourselves freed from jail, standing in the street. We looked at each other, not sure what to do next. After a moment Thaddaeus shrugged and said, "Let's go to the temple." So we entered the temple courts, just as the angel had commanded, and we began to "tell the people all about this new life."

I have already been telling you, my friend, about this 'new life' all during this story. And we had been telling the crowds at Solomon's Porch the same: this new life that is the resurrection life. Some call it resurrection power. This simply means learning to live with the same power that raised Jesus from the dead—Holy Spirit power.

This is the new life: a Holy Spirit powered life.

We call it resurrection power because when you are born again, it is as if you were resurrected from the dead. Because you were! The Spirit now indwells you and you are no longer the old you. A new power is at work. A power you never had before. Brother Paul says it like this:

"I have been crucified with Christ and I no longer live, but Christ lives in me. The life I now live in the body, I live by faith in the Son of God, who loved me and gave himself for me."

I ... me ... self ... King Peter ... no longer lives, but instead Jesus lives in me through the Holy Spirit. This new life is all about freedom, peace, joy, contentment, gratitude, and hope: confident expectation.

Freedom from and freedom to: freedom from the bonds and

prisons in which we have all put ourselves. And freedom to experience the fullness of God the Father's riches.

Peace – isn't this what we are all looking for – peace? A peace that comes from knowing my Father for who he is: all powerful, all-knowing, and all-loving. Because of this I learn to trust him completely, and therefore my life is saturated with power and peace, as though I am perfectly safe in his care … because I am …perfectly safe.

Joy – a joy that brings a pervasive sense of well-being; a sense deep in my soul that everything is okay, and everything will be okay. But more than just okay: immeasurably abundantly more than anything I can imagine, or even think to imagine.

Contentment – a contentment flowing naturally from this peace and joy. A contentment flowing from knowing "The LORD is my Shepherd and I shall not want for anything." I shall not. A contentment overflowing with the joy of Jesus, so I can say to all fears, anxieties and temptations, "No thanks, I'm full."

Gratitude – a gratitude that comes from knowing I was saved from the agony and suffering of Hell, but also saved from my Self, and the empty blind, lost, average life I was living. Oftentimes my prayers are simply, "Thank you, thank you, thank you!"

Hope – 'Hope' in the Scriptures means 'confident expectation.' A confident expectation that enables me to view any situation, no matter how unsettling, with so much confidence in the Holy Spirit power, I can sincerely say, "Thank you now, Father, for how you are going to work this out, because I know I will be thanking you later."

This is the new life about which the angel instructed us to tell the people. This is the new life you can have. I have it. It is amazing. I want you to have it, too.

> "What no eye has seen, what no ear has heard,
> and what no human mind has conceived" —
> the things God has prepared for those who love
> him—
> these are the things God has revealed to us by his
> Spirit.

29

Grace & Gratitude

We are moving towards Christmas and I want to pause, and think about how amazing this whole Jesus thing is. As we journey through life day to day we tend to get numbed by the morass of everyday living, and our senses become dulled. We take for granted the richness of life. We focus on our problems, our aggravations, and our anxieties, and we miss the incredible beauty and amazing magnificence of the Lord Jesus.

To be saved by Jesus is an amazing thing to consider, isn't it? This whole grace thing is simply amazing. Being adopted into God's family, being a child of God, now that is amazing!

If you get this, if you let this flow through you and over you, if you absorb this amazing grace, and are absorbed into it, you will be full of gratitude and joy. How could you not be?

Are you a grateful person? Have you ever thought about that? Do you typically move through the day filled with gratitude? Would those who know you think of you as someone who overflows with gratitude? Because that would have to be a wonderful indicator of a heart filled with joy, wouldn't it?

If you need a lift, what do you think about? When you are flat, and life is mundane, or you are in a dark place, and life is overwhelming, what can you think about to reboot and feel a sense of joy and gratitude? One avenue out of the flat life, or the dark heart, and into the Light is to remember what Jesus has done for you. And to constantly remind yourself you – you! – are a sinner saved by grace.

If you are born again, that is.

Jesus tells a story to drive home this point. He has been invited to Simon the Pharisee's home for lunch. Simon is a prude and stiff and I'm sure not much fun to be around. A "sinful" woman comes in and begins to weep at Jesus' feet, pouring perfume and washing them with her hair.

Simon's heart overflows with condescension and judgment, and he thinks to himself, "Humph, if Jesus was a true prophet, he would know this woman is a sinner." Now stop for a moment and think about what Simon just said: "This woman is a sinner." Which means ... he is sure he is not.

So Jesus says to Simon, "Two people owed their master money. One owed a bunch, the other not so much. The master forgave them both. Now which one do you think was the most grateful, Simon?"

The answer is obvious, isn't it? Jesus concludes with a description of Simon's heart: "But he who has been forgiven little loves little." Luke 7:36-50 Paraphrased

Have you been forgiven little or much? Do you realize what a lost and blind sinner you were? If so, how can anything but grace and gratitude overflow from your heart?

Or maybe you really think, deep down, that you were just not that bad. You might even think, although you would never say it, that it was a good day for the God team when you accepted Jesus' offer to join. It's not really amazing grace to you; it is perhaps just helpful grace. Or possibly just a polishing up kind of grace.

No. It's either amazing, or it's not true grace.

You don't *accept* Jesus into your heart, and you don't bless him by joining his team. You fall on your face and surrender your heart and your life to him. And if you truly have surrendered, and if you absorb, and keep absorbing this amazing miracle of his grace, your heart will be filled with gratitude, and streams of grace will start to flow from within.

But I must say, if it is not amazing to you, look deeply into the mirror of your heart. You don't want to take this for granted, and you sure don't want to miss this amazing gift of God's grace. A grateful person is a grace-full person, with a heart filled to overflowing with Light, brimming over with grace and joy.

Amazing.

Amazing Grace, how sweet the sound,
That saved a wretch like me....
I once was lost but now am found,
Was blind, but now, I see.

30

Dayenu

I am the luckiest person on the planet. I am.

Can you say this? And mean it?

If not I want to issue you a challenge: Why are you not?

If you do not feel this same way I encourage you to write down precisely why you *feel* – because it would all about your feelings – that you are not. My well-meaning friends often say I am blessed, not lucky, blessed being a more Biblical term. But I feel lucky every bit as much as I feel blessed.

I recently came across a Jewish Passover song, "Dayenu." Dayenu is sung during the Passover meal. Dayenu translates: "It would have been enough." Here is just a sampling. I have included the entire song at the end.

> If He had brought us out of Egypt, and had not
> carried out judgments against them – Dayenu, it
> would have been enough!
> If He had given us their wealth, and had not split the
> sea for us – Dayenu, it would have been enough!
> If He had split the sea for us, and had not taken us
> through it on dry land – Dayenu, it would have
> been enough!

Through this song my Jewish friends are making a practice of acknowledging everything God has done for them – already done for them – and realizing it is enough – more than enough. They are seeing that at any point if the Lord had stopped blessing them, it still would have been enough. More, in fact, than they ever deserved. Anything more is just icing on the cake.

Do you feel this way? I believe if you were to make a list of all the things the Lord has done for you, in so many various aspects of your life, you would be amazed at just how blessed ... lucky ... you are.

My desire, my purpose is to get you into the mindset of, "After all that Jesus has done for me – everything from this point forward is just icing on the cake."

To do this I might suggest you break this out into categories in your life such as:

Parents and the circumstances into which you were born and raised. (That would have been enough ... Dayenu!)

Having a spouse and/or having children. Your Health and the health of your family.

Having a job – a roof over your head – food to eat – a car to drive. For most of you it is a nice house ... good food ... a nice car .... Dayenu!

Perhaps try this:

Break your life into decades: 0-10 ... 10-20 ... 20-30 ... 30-40 ... and so on.

(I tried this and it took a while just to get out of my first decade.)

For each decade look back on the blessings you received. Were you born into a family with a house and food on the table – a family that loved you and cared for you? Dayenu.

Are you able to love someone, a family, friends – and be loved in return? Dayenu. Can you walk, talk, and read this, smell the roses, laugh and cry? Dayenu. Did you go to college? Dayenu. Do you have a job? Dayenu. Do you get to travel, even a little? Dayenu.

For each decade look back at what Jesus did for you in the good times: Dayenu. Then look at the bad times, and the good he brought out of them – often even the "immeasurably, abundantly more good than you could ask for, or even imagine to ask for."[1] Dayenu!

I am not trying to just upgrade your gratitude attitude, I am seeking to reset your entire perspective. For me, I want to not just look back and see all the Dayenu's in my life, but to have a perspective such that I am looking *forward* so that I see the Dayenu's as they come.

In fact, what I want is to live a life of Dayenu in every detail of every moment of every day. I want to see that I am *already* the luckiest man on the planet, and anything else is just Jesus lavishing me with more grace than I deserve. And I want to see that at any point, over all these years, Jesus could have stopped the blessings, and surely it would have been enough – way, way more than just enough.

For truly: "Jesus saved me from Hell. Everything after that is just icing!"

Dayenu!

Dayenu
If He had brought us out from Egypt,
    and had not carried out judgments against them
    — Dayenu, it would have been enough!
If He had carried out judgments against them,
    and not against their idols
    — Dayenu, it would have been enough!
If He had destroyed their idols,
    and had not smitten their first-born
    — Dayenu, it would have been enough!
If He had smitten their first-born,
    and had not given us their wealth
    — Dayenu, it would have been enough!
If He had given us their wealth,
    and had not split the sea for us
    — Dayenu, it would have been enough!
If He had split the sea for us,
    and had not taken us through it on dry land
    — Dayenu, it would have been enough!
If He had taken us through the sea on dry land,
    and had not drowned our oppressors in it
    — Dayenu, it would have been enough!
If He had drowned our oppressors in it,
    and had not supplied our needs in the desert for

forty years
 — Dayenu, it would have been enough!
If He had supplied our needs in the desert for forty
 years,
  and had not fed us the manna
   — Dayenu, it would have been enough!
If He had fed us the manna,
  and had not given us the Shabbat
   — Dayenu, it would have been enough!
If He had given us the Shabbat,
  and had not brought us before Mount Sinai
   — Dayenu, it would have been enough!
If He had brought us before Mount Sinai,
  and had not given us the Torah
   — Dayenu, it would have been enough!
If He had given us the Torah,
  and had not brought us into the land of Israel
   — Dayenu, it would have been enough!
If He had brought us into the land of Israel,
  and not built for us the Holy Temple
   — Dayenu, it would have been enough!
    — Dayenu, it would have been enough! dayenu!

---

[1] Ephesians 3:20

31

Amazing Grace

Through many dangers, toils and snares...
we have already come.
T'was Grace that brought us safe thus far...
and Grace will lead us home.

Are you a grateful person?

I'm grateful for all God has done for me, and for the blessings he has lavished upon me. Yes I am. But I am even more grateful for God's grace. Do you think about God's grace often? Because it is truly an amazing thing to ponder.

Grace is getting what you do not deserve: Grace is God's un-merited favor.

Did you know Jesus never uttered the word grace – not once? He just lived it. And died it. For you. So you could experience it. You. Flawed, prideful, judgmental, self-absorbed and selfish you: are loved, tenderly and adoringly by God Almighty, El Shaddai, creator of the universe.

Now that is amazing.

But the writers of the New Testament spoke a lot about grace. And their gratitude was overwhelming, and therefore overflowing. It's as if they felt like Jesus had freed them from prison.

If you have surrendered your life to Jesus, you are saved. Which means Jesus plucked you out of a prison with a death sentence hanging over your head, took your blame, absorbed your shame, and reconciled you with God.

Amazing.

I was talking with a friend recently who had actually been to prison. We were talking about how much she has grown spiritually, and how much Jesus has transformed her heart. You see, my friend had gotten caught up in a lifestyle that was not "walking in the Light." One thing led to another, and she was sentenced to seven years in prison. She is from a nice family and had a nice family of her own. (Please feel free to cast the first stone ...)

I asked her if she ever allowed herself to think about what it was like in prison, or did she have to block that completely from her mind? She said, "Oh no, I think about it all the time. And," she continued, "this may surprise you, but I think about how grateful I am, all the time."

Perplexed, I asked, "Grateful that you're out, and free?"

She replied, "Well, yes, of course. But I'm also grateful for going to prison. You see, Sam, I was in a different kind of prison before I went to prison."

Oh my.

"I was in a different kind of prison before I went to prison."

Now, as you are reading this, some of you are lighting up, and joining her with a resounding, "Yes, me too! I know just what you mean." Others of you are cynical, thinking, "Oh, another jailhouse conversion."

Some of you are thinking, "Well, I'm not perfect, but in prison? Oh come on, that's for you 'gutter to glory' types." Which can only mean ... you still are ... in prison.

The Apostle Paul joins my friend with overflowing gratitude for being rescued from his own prison:

> We always thank God, the Father of our Lord Jesus Christ ... **For he has rescued us from the dominion of darkness and brought us into the kingdom of the Son he loves,** in whom we have redemption, the forgiveness of sins." (Col. 1 bold added)

Rescued. Redeemed. The dominion of darkness. The kingdom of Light.

Forgiven.

Grace.

Amazing

32

Confident Expectation

During WWII, Hitler's henchmen employed various tech-niques to interrogate and ultimately break POWs. If they failed, their last ploy was to arrange for the soldier to escape. After the soldier was away from the POW camp and starting to believe he could actually make it to freedom, the SS would capture him again.

This broke the spirit of the soldier. He had found new hope but then lost it. His strength and resistance were shattered.

Hope is the glue that holds our joy together in the midst of trials. Did you get that? Hope is the glue that holds our joy together. Just as temptation is the bridge from joy to fear to sin, hope is the roadblock on that slippery bridge. Without hope, life is full of anxiety, contaminated with fear and is, well, slippery.

The movie, *The Big Chill*, opens with Alex having committed suicide. At the funeral, the southern pastor, in his gentlemanly drawl, asks, "Where did Alex's hope gooooo?"

> Be joyful in hope, patient in affliction, faithful in prayer. (Rom. 12:12)

How? A positive mental attitude? A wishing for the best? No. These are mere band aids.

Hope in the biblical language means "confident expectation." It's not wishful thinking. It's not "Gosh, if only…" Instead, it's "I'm not sure what God is going to do in this, but I'm absolutely sure of him and his perfect love."

Oswald Chambers called this being "certain in our uncertainty."[1]

Our hope, our confident expectation, is not in specific outcomes, specific timing, or in getting *our way*. Instead, our hope is in his perfect love, his total control over every situation that comes at us, and yes, even in his perfect timing.

When we place our confident expectation in the perfect love of our Heavenly Father, we are building our house of faith (trust) on rock... bedrock. And the deeper we drive our foundation anchors into that bedrock of his perfect love, the more unshakable is our trust. Our circumstances may or may not change; that is not the issue. Our hearts will change, and with that change, our trust will overflow, and we will not just "grit our teeth and get through it." We will soar through the problem.

> But those who hope in the LORD will renew their strength. They will soar on wings like eagles; they will run and not grow weary, they will walk and not be faint.
> (Isa. 40:31)

Even the muck of ordinary, day-to-day living loses its bite when viewed through the prism of confident expectation.

The Samaritan woman at the well must have lost all hope. Five husbands? No doubt, she was an outcast in her village. No chance for a future... no reason to hope. But an encounter with Jesus changed all of that.

> Jesus answered her, "If you knew the gift of God and who it is that asks you for a drink, you would have asked him and he would have given you living water." "Sir," the woman said, "you have nothing to draw with and the well is deep." Jesus answered, "Everyone who drinks this water will be thirsty again, but whoever drinks the water I give him will never thirst. Indeed, the water I give him will become in him a spring of water welling up to eternal life." (John 4:10-14)

Can't you just see her looking at this seemingly ordinary man and then looking down at the deep well? Imagine her feeling the pain of her hopeless situation, looking back at Jesus and saying, "The well of my lost hope is too deep for you to help me. And you don't even have a bucket! You can't change my circumstances."

I've said that to Jesus myself. "This is too complicated. *They* (or *it*) have the control. Even you can't help me with this."

In his reply, Jesus was telling the woman not to put her hope in ordinary water—in a change in her circumstances or human intervention—but to put her hope in his ability to change her heart and to bring joy in and through her trials. And with that kind of confident expectation placed in Jesus, not only would she regain her hope, her heart would overflow with newfound joy! A changed life.

> May the **God of hope** fill you with all joy and peace as you trust in him, so that you may **overflow with hope** by the power of the Holy Spirit. (Rom. 15:13 bold added)

Can Jesus do that for you? You better believe he can. He can do it "immeasurably, abundantly" more than anything you can ask for or even imagine asking for (Eph. 3:20). But only when we transfer our hope from our—or, someone else's—ability to change and/or control our circumstances to his ability to soar through the trials in our lives and place us on the rock of his hope.

---

[1] Oswald Chambers, *My Utmost For His Highest*, April 29.

33

Quicksand

Do you remember the old Tarzan TV shows? The safari crowd is moving through the jungle, and suddenly someone steps in the dreaded quicksand. "Don't wiggle around!" I shout at the TV... because everyone knows doing that will just make you sink faster.

Is there really such a thing as quicksand? Yes, and you don't have to go to Africa to get stuck in it. It's called the Past and the Future.

And if you move around too much in either one, you will surely sink faster.

As I was walking with my beloved Golden Retriever, Fannie, the other day, I was one with the world. It was late afternoon, my favorite time to walk. The sun was fading, the shadows were falling, and it was quiet. The Upstate South Carolina air was incredibly fresh, and I was vibrating at a high frequency.

Suddenly, a memory of something stupid I did years ago snuck into my Present. The dreadful Past. "What an idiot," it whispered to me. "A Christian? Ha!" the Past accuses me scornfully.

And, I'm stuck in quicksand.

If I want to "take hold of that for which Christ Jesus took hold of me" (Phil. 3:12), I'm going to have to let go of the Past. I'm going to have to let go of my own stupid, and yes, evil detours as well as what I perceive others have done to me.

But Satan will always seek to mire me in quicksand by reminding me and accusing me. Never forget his 3-D strategy: destroy, distract, and discourage. If he can keep you out of a saving relationship with Jesus, he will destroy your soul. Failing that, he will never stop trying to distract you and discourage you.

And he so often uses the Past and the Future. But you can let go of both of these because God is for you, God is with you, and God is before you. As recorded in Psalm 103:8-12, your Heavenly Father wants you to appropriate his divine forgetfulness into your Present:

> The Lord is compassionate and gracious, slow to anger, abounding in love. He will not always accuse, nor will he harbor his anger forever; he does not treat us as our sins deserve or repay us according to our iniquities... as far as the east is from the west, so far has he removed our transgressions from us.

"As far as the east is from the west?" Satan doesn't want you to hear about that.

One thousand years later, God was still reminding us of his unfailing forgetfulness as Paul assuages our fears about our Past:

> Once you were alienated from God and were enemies in your minds because of your evil behavior. But now he has reconciled you by Christ's physical body through death to present you **holy in his sight, without blemish and free from accusation...** (Col. 1:21-22, bold added)

When you surrendered and placed your full trust and dependence on Jesus, you were immediately washed clean of the Past. (You have surrendered, haven't you? If not, what in this world are you holding onto?)

God then dropped your sins into a deep abyss, and a No Fishing sign popped up.

Your Father never goes back fishing into that abyss to revisit your sins. Only you can do that.

So, stop it. Now! No fishing in the Past anymore.

Leave it there.
God has.

34

Intimacy

Since the light came on in 1995 (that means I was born again), my journey with the Lord has been a fascinating shift from the darkness into the light. I have encountered many ups and downs, with the ups always coming from God and the downs always—and I do mean always—coming from Sam.

One thing is for sure: I have changed. He has changed me. I began with Jesus becoming my Savior but only that: a Savior. Over the years, he has become more and more my Lord... as in, Lord over my life. But not *lording it over* my life. Instead, he has provided a steady flow of his goodness, grace, and love, washing over me and flowing through me.

He is now my Lord, my friend, my guide, my encourager, and even my accountability partner, gently convicting me when I start to drift away. How did I get here? And how can we both always be digging deeper, discovering more and more of the riches of his Kingdom?

Intimacy.

Intimacy develops through nourishing a relationship, not and never by just maintaining one.

Growing up as a child, God was a vague notion of some goodness and some badness... as in, punishment. After 1995, in my early years, my interaction with God was, at first, just that: an interaction with God... El Shaddai... this overwhelming cosmic power in the sky.

I mostly maintained an interaction—not a relationship—with fear and trembling. I didn't want to disobey this huge God because I didn't want him to be mad at me nor experience the bad consequences that would surely follow.

Consequently, there was absolutely no "life to the full" (John 10:10)

But as I grew, I started to see God in a different light: more goodness and grace than punishment. My perspective changed from not wanting to disobey God—so as to avoid bad consequences—to wanting to obey him but still mainly for the good consequences.

Still… a lot of maintenance and not much nourishment. And a shallow intimacy.

But then came another shift. It was slight at first, hardly noticeable to the outside world, but it was gathering steam toward a tectonic shift. I was changing, and my interaction with this huge God was shifting to a relationship with this intimate friend: my Savior, Jesus.

For intimacy to thrive, there must be transparency. And so, when I read with new eyes to see for the first time the following words of Jesus, I could sense the tectonic plates of my soul shifting:

> Whoever has my commands and obeys them, he is the one who loves me. He who loves me will be loved by my Father, and I too will love him and **show myself to him**. (John 14:21, bold added)

This was game-changing.

"…show myself to him."

Really? God himself, in the nature of the Son, Jesus, would become transparent with me so I could see him?

See him?

Jesus, the guy who rose from the dead, would show himself to *me*? Sinful, selfish, self-absorbed me?

Well, actually, no… not to the sinful, selfish, self-absorbed me but to the seeking, searching, surrendering me… the *me*, though still flawed, who was now seeing with more and more clarity this Jesus as someone with whom I could be intimate.

But was there a catch? "Whoever has my commands and **obeys** them, he is the one who loves me." Uh oh. Is this the catch? I have to obey—as in, be squeaky clean... or, at least, extra holy—to share this intimacy?

Well, again, no. Notice Jesus's words: "... he is the one who loves me." He didn't say, "When you obey me, you prove that you love me." Instead, he was saying, "You will obey me out of love for me because of our growing intimacy."

This sounds much more like a relationship. There's nourishment here, not just maintenance. There's transparency here, and intimacy thrives with nourishment and transparency.

Okay, but there actually is a catch: I can only *change* so much. Change is good, but this obedience from love is going to have to involve *transformation.*

What is the difference between change and transformation? Change is what I can do. Transformation is what God does in me.

Change to transformation.

35

A Present of the Present: Focusing on Today

Wherever you are, be all there.

– Jim Elliot

Satan will use the Past to mire us in quicksand, and he will use the Future to snatch away our Present. But God is assuring you he has both under control… because he is for you, he is with you, and he is before you… as promised through Isaiah:

> …for the Lord will go before you, the God of Israel will
> be your rear guard. (Isa. 52:12)

Your Heavenly Father wants you to "take hold of that for which Christ Jesus took hold of you" (Phil. 3:12), and you simply cannot take hold of anything while your hands are filled with the Past or the Future.

God promises… no, he *guarantees* you he has covered your Past because he is for you. He guarantees you he has the Future covered because he is always out before you. The only place he can be *with* you, though—and you, fully with him—is in the Present.

Imagine God saying to you, "I want to give a gift to you every day, my Child. What would you like?" (Which he does every day, by the way.)

The only sane answer would be, "You pick it, Lord."

And God just might say, "Okay, my first present to you is the Present. Because I cannot give you anything until you *take hold of* this gift."

Most of us are living everywhere but here... in the Present.

The martyred modern-day missionary, Jim Elliot, made this simple but profound observation: "Wherever you are, be all there."

How many times have I been in the midst of "taking hold of that"... the joy, the peace, the security, and the wholeness that flows from my time with Jesus when, without warning, the Future barges in uninvited, and the clouds of uncertainty roll in with it?

I start projecting out, and then the "what ifs?" and the "how will I evers?" come rushing in, stealing my joy and peace and taking captive the Present.

Jesus had a lot to say about not worrying about the Future. "Don't do it," he said. "And why would you?" he asked. "You can't do anything about it. And worrying about it won't help or change a thing" (Matt. 6:25-27).

Or... if we are not worrying about the future, we're daydreaming about it. "Life will be so much better when..."

If you miss everything I say today, please don't miss this: Never project out. Stop doing it as soon as you start. There is nothing good that can come from projecting out into the Future with "what ifs?" and "how will I evers?" You will most certainly not be accurate in your projections. Surely you know that you simply cannot know.

But God knows, and he is out before you.

So, as Jesus says, stop it. Don't do it.

Jesus, who knows your Father intimately, assures you that nothing—not one thing—will ever happen to you apart from the will of your Father (Matt. 10:29). He promises to you that God is always at work, never asleep at the wheel, and never preoccupied (John 5:17). So, you can stay in the Present, secure in the protection of his guarantee that he is with you. He has you "hemmed in" in the most precious of ways (Psa. 139:5).

The Present is the only place where you can live the "life that is truly life" (1 Tim. 6:19). The Present is the only place where you can experience the riches God has for you.

May you accept God's present of the Present and take hold of it... so Jesus can take hold of you.

36

No Fear in Love

The Lord does not give me rules, but He makes His stand-
ard very clear. If my relationship to Him is that of love, I will do
what He says without hesitation. If I hesitate, it is because I love
someone I have placed in competition with Him, namely, myself. —
Oswald Chambers[1]

My friend John recently said to me, "Sam, I'm really sweating
out this proposal I've submitted. I need to win this contract. I'll do
anything to get it, even bend the rules…slightly…if I have to. And I
may have to because my competitor is cutthroat. If I lose it, well,"
and he paused for a moment, "I just *can't* lose it! You're the preacher.
What do you have to say to help?"

John's eyes were darting around the room in a nervous frenzy,
and about every other word was a curse word. I hadn't seen him
this agitated in a while. So I tried to calm his nerves by quietly saying, "I would try to abandon the outcome to God, John, because you
do not control the outcome."

John's response: "But I'm afraid it might not be God's will that
I get this contract!"

And there it was. The core truth.

Oh my.

"I really don't want God's will…because I really do not trust
him."

How often do you obey—or, at least try to obey—but only out
of fear God might not give you what you want? Or perhaps try to
obey because of your fear of God's punishment if you displease

him? How often do you *act right*, motivated by fear of what other people might say about you? (Far too often.)

This kind of performance is all about fear.

Or, do you obey because you love God and trust him implicitly?

Jesus' dear friend, John, after a lifetime of watching Christians trying so hard to perform, motivated by fear, wrote,

> There is no fear in love. But perfect love drives out fear, because fear has to do with punishment. The one who fears is not made perfect in love.
> (1 John 4:18-19)

When we understand God loves us perfectly there is simply no room left in our hearts for fear: no fear of God, no fear of what others think, and no fear of…the outcome. His perfect love can and will drive out all your fears and fill your heart with so much trust that you will start to view fear as silly, useless, and totally illogical.

What a life this would be.

And you can have it.

But you will have to transfer your trust to Jesus.

---

[1] Oswald Chambers, My Utmost For His Highest, November 2.

37

Obedience out of Logic, Love, and Gratitude

Performance is fear-based. Obedience is love-based.
Performance is about points, as in accumulating enough points to earn the rewards we deserve. Obedience is about pleasing, as in pleasing my Heavenly Father.

As I have pondered my own transition from performance to pleasing, I see my three compelling reasons for seeking to obey my Heavenly Father are:

Love, Logic, Gratitude

Lavish Love

The first time I heard this passage read in church my heart jumped, and I was flooded with warmth:

> How great is the love the Father has lavished on us, that we should be called children of God! And that is what we are! (1 John 3:1)

Oh my, how great indeed is this love the Father has ... lavished on me ... you!

And Jesus perfectly captures the symbiotic relationship of commands, love, and obedience on his last night with his best friends:

> If you love me, you will obey my commands. (John 14:23)

Commands, yes. Obedience, yes. But all in and through love for my Savior. When I am compelled by his love for me, obedience replaces performance.

Logic

This one may seem counter-spiritual at first, but I seek to obey because, well, why wouldn't I? Do I think I know the best way to do things? Could I be such a moron as to want to set my own rules of behavior? I, and hopefully you, have learned the answer to these questions.

Peter sums this up perfectly when, after a particularly difficult teaching, Jesus asks the disciples if they want to leave him:

> "You do not want to leave too, do you?" Jesus asked the Twelve. Simon Peter answered him, "Lord, to whom shall we go? You have the words of eternal life. We have come to believe and to know that you are the Holy One of God." (John 6:67-69)

Peter, like me, and hopefully you, has tried running his life his way. We have gone elsewhere looking for the words of eternal life, and they are nowhere else to be found.

Gratitude

Luke tells the story about the overwhelming gratitude of a woman who "lived a sinful life," falling at Jesus' feet and washing his feet with her tears. When Jesus' host, Simon, turns his nose up at such base behavior, Jesus calls him out on it:

Then he turned toward the woman and said to Simon, "Do you see this woman? I came into your house. You did not give me any water for my feet, but she wet my feet with her tears and wiped them with her hair.

You did not give me a kiss, but this woman, from the time I entered, has not stopped kissing my feet.

Therefore, I tell you, her many sins have been forgiven—as her great love has shown. But whoever has been forgiven little loves little." (Luke 7:44-47)

Simon could have run theological circles around this woman. But he did not have what she had: love, exploding with gratitude.

If you want to live with joy power over sheer willpower—which surely you know by now doesn't work anyway—challenge yourself to examine why you do the things you do, the way you do them. Are you compelled to obey out of fear and performance, or out of love, logic, and gratitude?

One is a burden; the other a blessing.

38

I Want to See

Jesus asked him, "What do you want me to do for you?"
"Lord, I want to see," he replied.

—Blind Bartimaeus, Luke 18:40-41

As I was reading the accounts of Jesus' resurrection ap-
pearances I was struck by three encounters:

The first with the two men on the road to Emmaus that Sunday afternoon:

> When he was at the table with them, he took bread,
> gave thanks, broke it and began to give it to them. Then
> their eyes were opened and they recognized him ....
> (Luke 24:30-31)

The second when Jesus appeared to his disciples and friends later that evening:

> Then he opened their minds so they could understand
> the Scriptures. (Luke 24:45)

Ponder this for a moment. If you could ask Jesus for anything what would it be? What would you ask for? Would your requests be more about "for me," as "Do this for me," or "in me," as in "Do this in me, please?"

I wake up most mornings saying to Jesus: "Lord, I want to see. I want to see you, and I want to see as you see." And this is what caught my attention in these first two encounters.

Jesus opened the eyes of the two men so they could recognize him – so they could ... *see him* ... with the eyes of their heart. Later that evening he opened the eyes of his disciples so they could see the scriptures for the first time ... with the eyes of their heart.

Both encounters show us these men and women could see Jesus, as well as the scriptures, with the eyes in their head. But this is a far cry from seeing with the eyes of their heart. The difference is black and white versus color, seeing through a mirror dimly versus seeing with spiritual 20-20 vision. The difference is the fog of this tangible world versus the vivid clarity of the very real spiritual world.

The difference is just life, versus the life that is truly life.

Jesus had to open their eyes for them to truly see him for who he is, and to see the scriptures for what they say about him.

He has to do the same for you. You cannot achieve this. You have to want it.

Do you?

This is why I ask almost daily, "Lord, I want to see. I want to see you, and I want to see as you see." Could there be a richer gift? The more I see Jesus, in the details of my life, the deeper I will walk in the Kingdom, now. Not when I die. Now.

The more I see as Jesus sees, the more love, joy, peace and patience I will have. The more empathy and sympathy. The more clarity. The more compassion. The more wisdom. The more kindness. More grace and less judgment.

Jesus, please, I want to see.

Don't you?

I close with this prayer for you:

I pray that the eyes of your heart may be enlightened in order that you may know the hope to which he has called you, the riches of his glorious inheritance in the saints, and his incomparably great power for us who believe. (Ephesians 1:18-19)

39

Your Life as a Prize

I will give your life to you as a prize in all places, wherever you go.

—Jeremiah 45:5 NKJ

What a wonderful promise: "I will give you your life as a prize."[1]

My life is a prize. I hope yours is. Every day–yes, every day–I say, "I am the luckiest man alive." My well-meaning Christian friends are quick to suggest I say "blessed" instead of lucky, but I must tell you, I feel lucky. I feel like I have received a prize, and that prize is my Jesus-filled, joy-filled life.

Have you ever watched people at a sporting event react to the cheerleaders when they start throwing out t-shirts to the crowd? Grown men and women abandon all decorum and flail themselves about the stands trying desperately to catch these t-shirts. (Probably cheap cotton t-shirts at that!)

We love prizes, don't we? We feel so lucky when we win a prize. I vividly recall missing all the little plastic ducks at the fair when I was a little fellow, and as I turned away, dejected and forlorn, the man behind the counter handed me a little stuffed bear anyway.

I felt so lucky!

But not as lucky as having my life as a prize. A prize given to me by Jesus. How do you get this life? In the Old Testament God gives you a very clear process:

> Delight yourself in the Lord and he will give you the desires of your heart. (Ps. 37:4)

In the New Testament Jesus gives the same process:

> But seek first his kingdom and his righteousness, and all these things will be given to you as well. (Matt. 6:33)

To delight yourself in the LORD is to find your delight in Him, first and foremost. To delight yourself in the LORD is to seek Him first, to seek to live in His Kingdom first, here and now. To receive the desires of your heart you must abandon the cheap t-shirts of this culture and seek simple joy in Jesus. And the promise is that all these things–the desires of your heart–will be given to you.

"Okay," you say, "I hear that loud and clear. What is the catch?"

You do not know the desires of your heart. You simply do not. But He does.

You think you do, but how many times have you been sure something would bring you happiness, but it did not–not at all? Anyone who has lived long enough, and especially those who are seeking Jesus first, can attest to the fact, the absolute fact, that when they let go of actively flailing themselves after the cheap cotton t-shirts of the culture, Jesus gave them the desires of their heart.

And they will tell you they are so surprised to find they didn't have a clue what they would be.

But Jesus did.

Jesus gave them their life as a prize, and they now feel like they are the luckiest people on the planet.

But how to do this? How to receive the desires of your heart? Let go. Let go of what you are so sure will bring you happiness. Release the cheap cotton t-shirts of the culture and find your delight in Jesus–in his companionship; in his presence; in his deep, rich, love.

Release. Let go. In essence, abandon the outcome to Jesus.

Because you do not control the outcome. Let me repeat that for emphasis:

You, my friend, do not control the outcome–not in any way, not in anything. And it is your trying to control the outcome that is keeping you from experiencing your life as a prize.

So, relax, release, and abandon the outcome–and He will give you your life as a prize.

---

[1] *My Utmost for his Highest* April 28, Oswald Chambers

40

In the Flow of the Kingdom River

I am starting a deep dive study into the Sermon on the Mount. I hope you will join me. I think you will see Jesus' sermon in a fresh, new light. To get the full thrust I urge you to watch the YouTube videos at 721ministries.org.

Years ago, I joined some knucklehead friends rafting down the Chattooga River in Georgia. At times the river was easy and relaxing, and at times it was challenging, even a tad scary. (Not scary for me, of course, but for the others.) It was not just casual drifting; we had to do our part, keeping our paddles in the water to steer and navigate.

But here is the key – and the spiritual application: we were not operating in our own power. Our power source was the river. When we got out of the flow of the river we were back to operating in our power, paddling and working hard. At the end, the river dumped us into a big lake, across which we had to paddle to meet our ride. We quickly learned a raft is not made for lake paddling.

It was awful to be out of the flow of the river. Hard work. No fun. I kept expecting a Deliverance hand to slowly rise up out of the water. So today I want to talk about rivers: specifically the River of Life.

The Sermon on the Mount is all about living in the Kingdom of God now. Jesus wants you to know that you can live in the kingdom now. As Dallas Willard said, "If you want to go to heaven, go now."

To be frank, Jesus' teachings make little sense, and have little "real-world" relevance if not seen through his perspective of living in the Kingdom now. They are nice truisms and platitudes, and make for good bumper sticker and kitchen towel sayings. But oh, come on, no one is actually going to live them.

And please do not miss this: no one can live them outside the Kingdom.

But this Kingdom of God can be a vague and ambiguous concept. So today let me try to paint a picture that perhaps will be helpful. Let us start to think in terms of: "Life in the flow of the Kingdom."

The River of Life is throughout the biblical story. From Genesis to Revelation, we see the prophets and the psalmists repeatedly speaking of Living Water, and the River of Life. Jesus spoke often about this river and living water imagery.

To the Jews gathered in Jerusalem for the Feast of Tabernacles he declared:

> Let anyone who is thirsty come to me and drink. Whoever believes in me, as Scripture has said, rivers of living water will flow from within them. (John 7:37-38)

Can I get you to start thinking in terms of "Living in the flow of the Kingdom among us?" I can wrap my arms around that concept. We know what the flow of a river is like. I know when I am in the flow, and I know when I am not. Even more so, I know when the choice I am about to make is going to take me out of the flow.

You do, too.

The question is not, "Is this a sin?" or "Is this okay?" The better question is, "Is this in the flow of the Kingdom?" (Helpful hint: If you have to ask the question it's likely not.)

When I choose to get out of the flow it is as though I have gotten out of the raft and starting walking alongside the river by myself, while my buddies float on by. My feet are getting sore, I am getting tired and ornery. Trudging along, yes, trudging along in my own power – as I had done most of my life. Exhausting.

Where's the fun in that? Where is the power in that?

May you learn to stay in the flow of Jesus' Kingdom among us, and relish the ride.

41

Generous Eyes

You have heard that it was said to the people long ago, 'You shall not murder, and anyone who murders will be subject to judgment.' But I tell you that anyone who is angry with a brother – or neighbor - will be subject to judgment.

—Matthew 5:21

We have contrasted our mindset when trying to obey God: from "Lifeless to Better to Best." Trying to obey, that is, so as to stay out of trouble, or to gain his approval, or to feel good about ourselves, is lifeless. We can do better. We can live the best.

Today we move into Jesus' teaching on anger. Here is a personal example of my ... lifeless ... approach to anger. I decided years ago I would not do anything or say anything that would cause me to have to apologize later. That was my guardrail against anger.

And it works, for the most part. But it is not actually a guardrail against anger, is it? Instead, it is a guardrail against showing anger.

Surely you can see the lifelessness of such an approach. My entire motive is wrong. I don't want to show anger or act in anger because I do not want to have to apologize later. Why? Because my pride is such that I disdain humbling myself like that. I am too proud to apologize, so I will just avoid showing my anger.

This is exactly why Jesus taught us that the heart is the real issue, long before the action. My actions may be acceptable to the public, but my private heart is still a mess. A mess!

Perhaps a better approach would be to try not to get angry at all. Or not to sin in my anger. Apparently we can be angry and not sin. Jesus did, and we also read: "In your anger do not sin." (Ephesians 4:26)

But the plain truth is I have not done very well at not getting angry, and have failed completely at being angry and not sinning. And you? So let's seek to live the best life possible, instead of "Lifeless" or "Better." And a fine place to start would be with Jesus' own words:

> "The eye is the lamp of the body. If your eyes are generous, your whole body will be full of light. [23] But if your eyes are stingy, your whole body will be full of darkness. If then the light within you is darkness, how great is that darkness! (Matthew 6:22-23)

With generous eyes I practice viewing the other person in a light most favorable. I cut them some slack. I extend the grace I would want them to extend to me. (That would be the same grace I extend myself each time I act poorly, by the way). Jesus tells us that if our eyes are generous, our body will be full of light. But if our eyes are stingy and suspicious – and angry, our body will be full of darkness. And, "how great is that darkness!"

Viewing the other person in a light most favorable is looking at them, and whatever they did to raise your anger, with generous eyes. Maybe they are having a bad day. Or perhaps something very difficult is going on in their life. Or they just showed their fragile humanity and fumbled the situation. Or, maybe, just maybe, I am just being a big baby, whining because I did not get my way!

Generous eyes will also help us to first look in the mirror, as Jesus observed:

> Why do you look at the speck of sawdust in your brother's eye and pay no attention to the plank in your own eye? (Matthew 7:3)

If I first look in the mirror and see the huge plank-s in my heart, perhaps what at first seemed to my stingy eyes to be logs in the other person's life, will diminish to mere specks of dust by comparison. My anger will diminish with it.

Let's begin to practice these.

And yet these are only steps we can take to change our hearts. Transformation is the goal, and only Jesus and the Holy Spirit can do that. Therefore let us learn more and more to lean into and lean onto the Holy Spirit to soften our hearts. Someday soon we may *respond* to anger with a heart so averse to *reacting* in anger that we say, "Why would I drink that rat poison?"

That would be walking in the light with a generous heart, a heart after God's own heart. (1 Samuel 13:14)

42

Generous or Suspicious?

"So," Andrew continued, "We do our part to change, and the Spirit joins with us and does his part to transform us." And since you were asking about my big brother, one of the biggest transformations in Peter is his generosity. He used to be such a miser, counting every mite and denarius. But now he is indeed a different man.

"I know, because I know him better than anyone, having grown up with him, and worked with him for years. His heart has truly softened. He has so much more peace and so much more joy. His eyes, once stingy and suspicious, now shine with a twinkle of positive energy. It is an amazing thing to behold, having known big brother for so many years as an uptight grump."

Andrew paused and said, "Secundus, do you know what Peter's first thoughts were about Jesus?"

Secundus shook his head. Andrew burst out laughing and said, "He said, 'I wonder how long it will take Jesus to start asking for money?'"

Andrew watched Secundus' face frown in doubt. "Yes," he continued, "the great Peter, the First Apostle, Jesus' right-hand man, was originally suspicious of Jesus' motives. Of course he was, because he was suspicious of everyone's motives back then. He would rarely loan money to anyone, and even more rarely did he volunteer to help someone in need.

"He was closed off to the life around him, and was missing so much."

Secundus said, "Okay, that reminds me, we were going to discuss Jesus' words, 'The eye is the lamp of the body. If your eyes are good, your whole body will be full of light. But if your eyes are bad, your whole body will be full of darkness. If then the light within you is darkness, how great is that darkness!'"

"Oh yes, I almost forgot!" Andrew said, laughing. "I am sure Peter is a perfect example of what Jesus meant. You know Jesus actually said, 'If your eyes are generous,' not, 'if your eyes are good.' And instead of 'bad' eyes he said, 'If your eyes see double,' as in being suspicious and stingy."

"Okay, I see what you mean," Secundus said, nodding his head with understanding. "Before the Holy Spirit transformed Peter, he was stingy with his money, as you said, which led him to be suspicious of everyone's motives. Consequently he was often grumpy and tense and anxious, as even he now gladly admits."

"Yes, you got it my friend!" Andrew said, patting Secundus on the back. "He was all closed up back then. No real joy. Distracted and brooding most of the time. But now it is as though a warm, joyful light shines forth from within him. And I am convinced this is due in large part to the Spirit transforming his heart from stingy to generous."

"Wow," Secundus muttered, "I'm feeling a strong conviction about myself, and how stingy I used to be. But now, what a difference, Andrew. I now have 'the life that is truly life!' And I am so grateful the Holy Spirit opened my once dark eyes to the light of the truth: giving generously is the most freeing thing I can do!"

Andrew smiled and said, "Always remember this: Whoever sows sparingly will also reap sparingly, and whoever sows generously will also reap generously. Each of us should give what we have decided in our heart to give, not reluctantly or under compulsion, for God loves a cheerful giver. And God is able to bless us abundantly, so that in all things at all times, having all that we need, we will abound in every good work."

Part 3

Trials

43

It is So Simple: Follow Me

*When Peter saw him, he asked, "Lord, what about him?" Jesus answered, "If I want him to remain alive until I return, what is that to you? **You must follow me**."*

—John 21:21-22, bold added

We are back diving into the Gospel of John, as we finish our look at John 1:37-51. There are two principles in this passage dear to my heart:

1. For a disciple of Jesus the simple path is, "Follow me."

2. For a disciple the simple invitation to others is, "Come and see."

John the Baptist has just pointed Jesus out to young Andrew and John, (the writer of this gospel) and they start walking after him. Jesus turns around and asks them what is it they want with him, and in perhaps the all-time dumbest answer ever, they fumble out a lame,

They said, "Rabbi" (which means "Teacher"), "where are you staying?"

Now of all the options Jesus has at his disposal with which to answer them, including something sarcastic like, "Is that the best you can come up with?" – Jesus simply replies:

"Come," he replied, "and you will see."

John continues the story:

"The next day Jesus decided to leave for Galilee. Finding Philip, he said to him, "Follow me."

We make things so complicated, don't we? We get into discussions and debates and even arguments about details that serve only to distract us from what is most important: Following Jesus.

Notice in Jesus' invitation to both Andrew and John, as well as Philip, Jesus did *not* say, "Come sit over here and start taking notes about systematic theology."

He did not say, "I have a five point lecture on forgiveness, and following that a class on tithing, and following that we will discuss at length church doctrine and denominational mission statements."

He simply said, in essence, "Follow me ... first, and as you do you will see and understand all that I have for you."

Now you may be thinking, "Okay, those disciples literally followed a man named Jesus. They walked around with him, learning directly from him. What does that look like now, in my world?"

It looks like keeping your eyes focused on him first and foremost, especially when distractions and complications become clouding and confusing. It looks like following Jesus first, not first following your preacher, teacher, church, church doctrine or denomination.

It certainly looks like not following the culture around you – I hope that is a given.

For me, many times it looks like slowing down, and sitting with my best friend Jesus, simply by reading the "red ink" in the gospels. Simply reading Jesus' words. (I am constantly reading the whole of the scriptures, and yes all scripture is God-breathed, inspired, and of absolute equal importance.)

But there are times when just reading Jesus' words is so comforting, and so clarifying. The fog lifts and the way becomes clear. When I lose my way, or the way is uncertain, I simply slow down and follow Jesus as he says,

"I am the way and the truth and the life ... Follow me."
(John 1:6)

44

It is So Simple: Come and See

We are back diving into the Gospel of John, as we finish our look at John 1:37-51. There are two principles in this passage dear to my heart:

1. For a disciple of Jesus the simple path is, "Follow me."

2. For a disciple the simple invitation to others is, "Come and see."

Previously we reminded ourselves that when we are confused, or distracted, or harried and hurried, and not sure what being a "good Christian" looks like, a simple step is to slow down, and simply follow Jesus ... and his words.

But it does not always feel so simple, or easy to do, does it?

> When Peter saw him, he asked, "Lord, what about him?" Jesus answered, "If I want him to remain alive until I return, what is that to you? **You must follow me.**" (John 21:21-22 Bold mine)

Even Peter must be reminded – and rebuked – because he became preoccupied with John, and not Jesus. Jesus had just told Peter three times that his primary focus was to be on taking care of his followers: "Take care of my sheep." Yet astoundingly, Peter immediately loses his focus, forgets his mission, and starts wondering about what John's mission might be.

Jesus' response is meant for us all: "What is that to you? You must follow me."

Yes, Jesus, but what about all the Christian hypocrites? "What is that to you? You must follow me."

Okay, but what about the seven days of creation? And how did all the animals fit in the ark?

"What is that to you? You must follow me?"

What about predestination versus free will?

What about infant baptism versus immersion?

What about all the bad things done in the name of religion?

What about all the errors and contradictions critics claim are in the Bible?

What about ... What about ... What about ...? – You fill in your own blank, but the answer is the same:

"What is that to you? I may make those things clear to you and I may not. But you must follow me."

Now, many people you know who are not following Jesus have similar questions. For them your simple invitation is, "Come and see."

"Just come and meet Jesus." This is what Philip said to Nathaniel when he stiff-armed, and even questioned Jesus' character.

> "Nazareth! Can anything good come from there?"
> Nathanael asked. "Come and see," said Philip." (John
> 1:46)

I have encountered many men and women who have objections, and even sincere questions similar to these above. I feel confident I can answer most of their questions – that is, if they really want an answer.

But I am even more confident that if they will "come and see Jesus," two things will happen:

As they get to know Jesus they will like him. Really like him.

And they will be surprised when they realize how much he likes them. Really likes them.

And really likes you.
Not sure about that? Just come and see.

45

Israel Trip: Pass—Fail

My wife Dina and I just returned from eight days on the ground in Israel. We were with a tour group and each morning our leader and teacher would ask for prayer requests. Please forgive my, perhaps glaring spiritual weakness, but I rapidly lose interest praying for someone's aunt's best friend in Indiana, who is going through a hard time.

There, I said it.

The coronavirus had prevented us from visiting Bethlehem. Reports stated there were several unlucky Americans quarantined for two weeks in a hotel room because they had visited Bethlehem – stuck in their rooms for fourteen days.

I felt so sorry for them, and, was just so glad we were not in their shoes.

Oh, how little did I know, and how little did I know I was about to fail a big test.

It was early morning of our last day in Israel. We fly out in twenty-four hours. I was ready to get home! We were gathered at the entry gate to the Temple Mount. I was so very excited to actually walk around this ancient site that Herod the Great had built during Jesus' lifetime. Jesus would have walked around these very grounds many times.

I am feeling very spiritual and in the moment, when our leader says, "Since we have a bit of a wait before we will be admitted to the site, are there any prayer requests?" I took a deep breath and hummed a few Zen notes, bracing for the "please pray for my aunt in Idaho's sister's marriage problems," when the lady next to me started sobbing and blurted out, with tears flowing and nose running:

"My parents' best friend died last night of the coronavirus, and they think my parents gave it to him. And my grandchildren live next door to my parents and visit and play with them all the time. I am so worried for them!"

Okay, that is a serious prayer request, worthy of compassion and care and love. But before I could fully process her words she continued:

"And ... I visited my parents right before I came on this trip."

Group silence. Hearts sinking. Slowly her words, and their implication, dawned on me. I put my head in my hands and thought to myself, "She didn't just say what I think she just said, did she? She didn't just rat us out to the world that we may have all just spent eight days – on a bus – with a coronavirus carrier?"

Our American and our Jewish leader conferred, and then said, "We have to report this. It would be unethical not to."

At that moment I was all for being as unethical as necessary.

The response of the Israeli government: Two week quarantine. Fourteen days. (No exercise, run out of books to read, terrible beds, terrible food.)

Now I am sure Jesus would have wanted me to love on this lady, and hug her, and tell her she is not to blame, and that we care for her and stand with her, and we are all brothers and sisters in Christ –and all that.

I failed that test with prejudice.

There was not a loving, Christian bone in my body at this point. I tried to talk to Jesus. I tried to ask the Holy Spirit for guidance, and love and compassion. For a soft, forgiving heart. But my heart was so hard my prayers felt like they were rattling around inside a dark, stone cavern.

Our leader then said, with conviction, "Friends, either God is in charge or he is not."

Well my friend, I teach this all the time. I believe it. I live by it. You've heard me many times: "God is in the details – your details.

He loves you perfectly; he is perfectly present; he is perfectly powerful. Jesus will never forsake you."

But for the next several hours I was a practicing atheist – not in my head, but in my heart. I failed on every level: as a Christian, as a follower of Jesus, as a teacher and a minister of the Word.

Perhaps you have had a similar experience?

I could only find comfort in the Holy Spirit's words through Paul:

> Therefore, there is now no condemnation for those who
> are in Christ Jesus. (Rom. 8:1)

I failed, but I am forgiven. I failed, but I am still loved – adored, actually. I failed, but I am still in the Kingdom and still in the Family.

No condemnation, only conviction. Conviction from the Holy Spirit that, "Sam, you can and you must do better next time."

Oh, by the way, after six excruciating hours, we were told that since our friend had no symptoms, and it had been fourteen days since her visit to her parents, we could go home.

A miracle? Certainly not because of my prayers, we can rest assured of that!

46

When 31-7 is
Not the Final Score

Okay, I am watching the Stanford – Oregon football game
a while back with my bride and suddenly I get a high-beam from
the Holy Spirit. Allow me to explain.

At halftime Oregon is leading 24-7 and they are dominating
Stanford all over the field. The Oregon home field crowd is loud and
raucous. Clearly it is not Stanford's night, and just as clearly this
game is no longer worth watching.

We go to sleep. (But I did record the game, just in case.)

Sunday I check all the Saturday college scores and I see, much
to my shock and dismay, Stanford won the game in overtime, 38-31.
I have no choice but to watch the second half to see how this could
have possibly happened.

But with only 4:47 minutes left in the 3rd quarter the score is still
24-7, and Oregon is driving toward the end zone. The crowd is still
just as loud and raucous, and Oregon is still dominating the game.
I keep looking at Dina and saying, "How in the world is Stanford
going to come back from this? Someone must have printed the final
score incorrectly."

As if to pile on the sheer impossibility of any comeback, 15 seconds later Oregon scored again to go up 31-7. Now of course there
is just no feasible way Stanford is going to come back and win this
game. Not unless a miracle happens.

And that is when the Holy Spirit spoke.

You see I knew the final score. I knew Stanford had come back and won. It didn't matter how bad it got. The crowd could get louder and louder; the referees could blow an important call; the score could even get worse. None of that could rattle me.

I knew the outcome.

And as a follower of Jesus Christ, you do too.

Imagine I am a rabid Stanford football fan and I am watching this all unfold, yet knowing the outcome as I do. What would be my thoughts ... my emotions? Would I be full of fear and anxiety? Would I be about to collapse? No, I would actually be enjoying the game. And the worse it got the more my joyful anticipation would grow.

I know the outcome.

If you are a follower of Jesus, 31-7 is never the final score. If Jesus is your Savior and Lord, there will always be a comeback. He will always bring good out of every 31-7. The good is not always our preconceived idea of the good, but it is always immeasurably, abundantly more that we could ask, or even imagine to ask.

John tells the story in his gospel of a certain royal official coming to Jesus to heal his dying son. It is 31-7 for this man and his son. But Jesus says to him, "You may go. Your son will live." (John 4:50)

Then: "The man took Jesus at his word and departed."

He took Jesus at his word. He simply took Jesus at his word.

Do you?

We complicate this whole religion thing with all kinds of distractions. Perhaps we should all just "take Jesus at his word and depart" — from whatever is worrying us.

Jesus gives you his word about his perfect love, his perfect control over your life, and his perfect knowledge of all the details of your life. Yes, all. He knows when it's 31-7.

He has given us his word through so many promises, but I will leave you with just one:

> "So do not worry, saying, 'What shall we eat?' or 'What shall we drink?' or 'What shall we wear?' For the pagans run after all these things, and your Heavenly Father knows that you need them. But seek first his

kingdom and his righteousness, and all these things will be given to you as well." (Matt. 6:31-33)

47

The 3 You's

This chaos in our country is the perfect scenario for Satan to advance his strategy to destroy the "Life to the full" Jesus promised you could have. It is his breeding ground to distract you from "The life that is truly life" Jesus died for you to have. And if you allow the chaos in our country to become the discouraging chaos in your soul, Satan is winning and laughing.

Do not let him.

Jesus offers simpler answers:

1. "What is that to you? You must follow me."
2. "Who do you say I am?"
3. "You are the man!"

For the past three Putting Greens we have been seeking to divert our focus from the externals of our world to the internals of our souls. The externals of this world are like the shifting sands of the temporal, here today – shifting tomorrow, but your internal soul is eternal. This is so important I want to summarize all this with a fourth Putting Green.

To frame our perspective, let us return to our original questions:

Is the United States eternal?

Are the Democrats and the Republicans eternal?

Is China eternal?

Is this pandemic eternal?

Is the media – the stock market – the upcoming election – Trump Biden – Antifa – riots – economic collapse ... eternal?

But most pertinent: Are you?

The answers: All no's and the last a big yes.

Why the 3 You's? Because it always comes down to you – and your life with Jesus. Not your pastor, your spouse, your favorite Bible teacher, your Sunday School class friends. You.

I am going to make a broad, sweeping declaration which I am wont to do: If we focused on these 3 You's whenever we are wobbling and worrying, our lives would be enlightened with a light and a life-giving clarity.

Amidst all the chaos in our country – and perhaps in your personal life as well – Jesus is saying to you and to me:

1. "You do not need to worry about all this chaos, nor the election, nor those people who offend and frighten you. Keep your focus on me."

2. "When your faith wobbles because your feelings are taking over, just remember, 'Who do you say I am?' Because if I am who you say I am, then ... Keep your focus on me."

3. And when you are so sure that whatever problem you have is about someone else's actions or behavior, just remember, it is not about them, it is about you, and you and Me, because ... You are the man; You are the woman, I care about right now."

As Peter stated so succinctly:

Cast all your anxiety on him because he cares for you.
(1 Pet. 5:7)

And he does, you know.

I want to leave you with the words of Eugene Peterson's daughter at his funeral:

The simple secret you taught me, Dad, every day of my life is this:

    God loves you.
    He is on your side.
    He is coming after you.
    He is relentless.

48

I Love Adversity?

I do not like adversity. I think my top goal each day is to avoid discomfort of any kind. I like things to go my way. I like things to work out nicely—for me, and for everyone who matters to me. So yes, I must confess, comfort is an idol for me.

But too much comfort makes for a soft Sam. Too much comfort makes for a passive Sam. Too much comfort makes for a spoiled Sam. Too much comfort makes for a "King of his Castle" Sam.

We have been looking at Solomon's words in Ecclesiastes, and how, looking back, he found his life to be so meaningless. You may think Solomon was a great king, but he was perhaps the worst king in the history of Israel. Does this surprise you? Just consider this:

> As Solomon grew old, his wives turned his heart after other gods, and his heart was not fully devoted to the LORD his God, as the heart of David his father had been. He followed Ashtoreth the goddess of the Sidonians, and Molek the detestable god of the Ammonites. So Solomon did evil in the eyes of the LORD; he did not follow the LORD completely, as David his father had done. (1 Kngs. 11:4-6)

What a collapse; what a fall from grace. And why? At least partly because he never faced any pain or adversity. Solomon, it turns out, was a sorry, stupid king. He was soft, he was passive, he was spoiled, and he was most definitely "King of his obscenely large Castle."

If you read about Solomon's life, he faced practically no adversity. He inherited the power and the peace of his father David's kingdom. David had done all the fighting for him. He inherited the riches of David's kingdom, because his father had done all the fighting for him.

Recently I decided to get back into at least some strength training. So I signed up with a personal trainer. He immediately put me through a challenging program of weightlifting with 1 # barbells. He made me do 2 pushups and 5 sit-ups at a time!

Oh come on, no one will grow stronger like that. We must challenge our bodies, at least to some degree. I am no longer a prisoner to the, "No pain no gain" approach, but we obviously will not grow without adversity.

This is why Peter would say:

> In all this you greatly rejoice, though now for a little while you may have had to suffer grief in all kinds of trials.

And why?

> These have come so that the proven genuineness of your faith—**of greater worth than gold**, which perishes even though refined by fire—may result in praise, glory and honor when Jesus Christ is revealed. (1 Pet. 1:6-7, bold added)

This is why James, Jesus' little brother, would say:

> Consider it pure joy, my brothers and sisters, whenever you face trials of many kinds ...

And why?

> ... because you know that the testing of your faith produces perseverance. Let perseverance finish its

work so that you may be mature and complete, not lacking anything. (Jas. 1:2)

This is why the writer of Hebrews would say:

My son, do not make light of the Lord's discipline, and do not lose heart when he rebukes you,
(Heb. 12:5)

And why?

... because the Lord disciplines the one he loves, and he chastens everyone he accepts as his son.
(Heb. 12:6)

Therefore:

Endure hardship as discipline; God is treating you as his children. For what children are not disciplined by their father? If you are not disciplined—and everyone undergoes discipline—then you are not legitimate, not true sons and daughters at all.
(Heb. 12: 7-8)

And why?

... God disciplines us for our good, in order that we may share in his holiness. No discipline seems pleasant at the time, but painful. Later on, however, **it produces a harvest of righteousness and peace for those who have been trained by it.** (Heb. 12:10-11, bold added)

Yes, later on it absolutely will produce a harvest of righteousness and peace—which is what we all are searching for, whether we know it or not. And it will bring you closer to Jesus—which is what we all are searching for, whether we know it or not—when you turn your focus from your pain, to your best friend and Savior.

Therefore I encourage you to, consider it pure joy, my brothers and sisters, whenever you face trials of many kinds. Use it as training for an overflowing harvest of righteousness and peace.

49

Sifted

Is Satan running the show down here on earth or does he have limits to his power? Can he do as he pleases, or is God in control? Yes, he has limits and yes, God is in absolute control. In fact, he has Satan on a leash. Even so, at times he allows Satan to sift us.

We cannot understand all the whys and hows, but we can catch a glimpse into this cosmic conundrum by observing both Peter's and Job's experience. (We will look at Job next week) In both cases, Satan must ask permission to attack these men. There is comfort in this Satan-on-a-leash concept, but it still leaves us uneasy as to the why, so let's dig deeper.

Peter is a favorite character in the Bible. The difference between the Peter we see before he was sifted and the Peter after he was sifted is startling. Before he is sifted, we see an impetuous, bragga-docios, prideful, can-do man. He's smart-mouthed, quick-mouthed, loud-mouthed, and foot-in-mouthed.

He reminds me of ... (hopefully the old) me.

"I'll walk on water, but I forgot my life-preserver. I'll stand by you, Jesus, till death, but I cannot seem to stay awake tonight. I will fight the world with my sword for you Jesus, but oops, I only got an ear."

What a guy!

The Peter we see after sifting is a kind, gentle, reflective, and patient man of God:

Above all, love each other deeply, because love covers over a multitude of sins.[1]

God opposes the proud but gives grace to the humble. Humble yourselves, therefore, under

God's mighty hand ...[2]

Simon Peter, a servant ... of Jesus Christ.[3]

What happened to bring about such a radical change? Where did all his baggage go? What softened big, tough, braggadocios Peter?

He got sifted.

On the final night Jesus spent with his closest friends, he warns Peter (Simon) of an impending trial:

"Simon, Simon, Satan has asked to sift you as wheat."[4]

Now if I'm Peter, I'm hoping, and even expecting, the next words out of Jesus' mouth to be, "But no need to worry, Peter. I have denied Satan and I will protect you from any distress."

And I'd be disappointed. Instead,

> "But I have prayed for you, Simon, that your faith may not fail. And when you have turned back, strengthen your brothers."[4]

"You have prayed ...for what? For my faith not to fail? Jesus, please forget praying and start protecting!"

But Jesus knew then what we all learn sooner or later: We are all carrying a lot of baggage, as well as clinging to idols, many of which we are not even aware. Jesus knows we need his help getting rid of this baggage, as well as the idols. We simply cannot free ourselves from either on our own.

They cling to us, and we cling to them. So I need sifting and so do you. I have been following Jesus for twenty-seven years, and I still need sifting. I want all that negative stuff gone, and I cannot seem to do it myself. Yes, I can self-sift, and I seek to. But for the really sticky stuff, I need Jesus' help.

And so do you.

---

[1] 1 Peter 4:8
[2] 1 Peter 5:5-6b
[3] 2 Peter 1:1
[4] Luke 22:31-32

50

Shaken Not Stirred

Although the Lord gives you the bread of adversity and the water of affliction, your teachers will be hidden no more; with your own eyes you will see them.

—Isaiah 30:20

Previously we saw that Jesus allowed Peter to be "sifted as wheat" – by Satan. He allows this because he knows Peter has accumulated baggage over the years, baggage that needed shedding. Jesus knew that Peter, like all of us, was either clinging to, or being clung to, by a host of idols, false bravado, pride, selfishness, hurt, fear, dysfunctional coping mechanisms and control issues.

Jesus knows the idols and illusions you and I are clinging to, and he knows the baggage clinging to us. And he knows we will not give them up easily. Often, we don't even see the harm they are causing. We're so busy and we're so distracted, we are blind to our silly illusions and our puny idols. Idols we are so sure we must have to be happy.

So as a favor to us – yes a favor – God allows troubles to stir us up. He uses trials to shake us up, so we can wake up from our cultural stupor. It appears God lets Satan do some of this work for him, using him like a tool, for our good. Perhaps our loving Father allows us, and others around us, to cause the trouble, as well.

I was once in a severe ditch, so I called my wise friend Det, and explained the situation to him. I then asked, "Do you think this is from God or from Satan? It would help me cope if I knew."

His answer, "Yes."

Does it really matter who and what? God is not doing this *to* you, but rather he is working through the brokenness of this world to accomplish something far greater *in* you. If you will let him. Do not miss that: If you will let him.

Picture this: there you are, covered with all sorts of negative thoughts, fears, false illusions, and silly idols. God allows you to be put into a sieve and the sifting process begins. Uh oh, you're being bumped around and it hurts. "I don't like this, God!"

But look, a false idol just fell off. And there, a bad habit and a negative emotion you've been harboring just shook off. Yes, that false bravado and foolish pride finally tumbled away. An illusion that, "I have to have this to be happy," just fell away. And a persistent lust disappeared.

There goes a control issue, and a bit of your ego, even that unpleasant competitive streak – all sifting off until you are free. And typically the last to sift away: "My claim to my right to myself."[1]

And finally, you can start to see. You can start to see your true Self, and you can also begin to see the true Father.

Job, who was described by God as, "blameless and upright," had this to say after his own sifting experience:

> "My ears had heard of you, but now my eyes have seen you."[2]

Yes, God described Job as a righteous man. But he still had so far to go in his spiritual journey. After Job's sifting experience he is now a man who is free from his old Self and can now see the real God. With his newfound 20-20 spiritual vision, he even says this about himself:

> My ears had heard of you
> but now my eyes have seen you.

Therefore I despise myself
and repent in dust and ashes.[2]

Is this new clarity and freedom worth the painful sifting? Peter and Job, and many of us, would declare, "Yes!"

---

[1] Oswald Chambers
[2] Job 42: 5-6

51

There's a Thorn in My Side

Therefore, in order to keep me from becoming conceited, I was given a thorn in my flesh, a messenger of Satan, to torment me.

—2 Corinthians 12:7

Peter was sifted. His loving Father knew he was con-trolled by Self ... aka King Peter, and needed to be sifted to be freed. Job was sifted as well. He was righteous, but his loving Father knew he was still blind to the deeper richness awaiting him, of knowing God more intimately.

The Apostle Paul found himself living with a thorn in his side. As the negative effects of this thorn progressed from frustrating, to aggravating, to out and out painful, we see Paul himself progress: from pleading with God to take it away, to thanking God for the thorn.

Thanking God for his thorn? Is Paul a masochist? No. And it is not his personality type that is important for us to understand; it is the progression he experienced as he moved from irritation to despair to delight.

For you and for me, the question to ask is, how did Paul, and therefore how do we, reach a place in our spiritual journey where we see God's thorns as the helpful gifts He intends them to be?

Don't miss that: How do you progress from whining and complaining to God about the things and the people you don't like in your life, to seeing through a lens of God's perfect power, his perfect love, and his perfect plan for you?

Let's first define our terms: A thorn is anything, or perhaps more applicable, any *one*, in your life who is causing you frustration, irritation, even pain. You don't want this thorn, you don't like this thorn, and you cannot control it, nor can you fix it. We don't like things we cannot control, and we certainly do not like things – or people – we cannot fix.

There are many types of thorns. Perhaps yours is a troublesome family member, or a wife or husband who just won't … do right, or a person from your working world. Maybe it's a physical issue, a monetary issue, or a marriage issue.

I find it interesting we are not told specifically what Paul's thorn is. My guess is if we were told, we would say, "Well, that is his, not mine. Mine is different. So, Paul's response doesn't apply to me. Besides, mine is worse."

Paul pleaded three times for God to take his thorn away. We have the advantage of seeing Paul's perspective after he has processed through his thorn problem, and moved from whining and complaining and pleading to God, to the clarity of seeing it as a tool and a gift his loving Heavenly Father is using to strengthen him.

Paul brings us directly to his issue: "Therefore, in order to keep me from becoming conceited …."

Maybe this conceit issue does not apply to you, so you can stop reading now. But if conceit, or Self-reliance, or "If I don't, it won't – If it's to be it's up to me," can at times describe you, then read on.

Paul knew himself well. He knew if God removed this thorn, he would likely drift back towards Self-reliance, and away from total reliance on God. He also knew when he acted in his own power, relying on his Self, the results would be a C- at best. Perhaps more likely a D to an outright F.

So Paul states unequivocally, "Therefore I will boast all the more gladly about my weaknesses, so that Christ's power may rest on me."

Christ's power, not mine. Jesus' Holy Spirit power resting on me and energizing me, not my power. My power, in the long run, is weak, compared to the incredible power of the Holy Spirit acting in and through me.

52

There's a Thorn in My Side
Part 2

---

*Therefore, in order to keep me from becoming conceited, I
was given a thorn in my flesh, a messenger of Satan, to torment me.*

—2 Corinthians 12:7

We have already asked the question: How do you pro-gress from whining and complaining to God about the things and
people you don't like in your life, to seeing through a lens of God's
perfect power, his perfect love, and his perfect plan for you?

We begin with the understanding that God's perfect plan is to
conform us to the likeness of Jesus. (Romans 8:29) That is very good
news, but this conforming process clearly must involve thorns.
Why? Paul gives us two reasons:

> … in order to keep me from becoming conceited.
> (2 Corinthians 12:7)

> Indeed, we felt we had received the sentence of death.
> But this happened **that we might not rely on ourselves
> but on God**, who raises the dead.

(2 Corinthians 1:9 Bold added)

Maybe you are not at all like Paul. Perhaps you have no issues with conceit. But I do not have to know you personally to know you tend to rely on Self, instead of relying on Jesus. How do I know this? You are human, and you are American.

I now understand what the Holy Spirit is saying through Paul, when Paul arrives at this poignant conclusion:

> Therefore I will boast all the more gladly about my weaknesses, so that Christ's power may rest on me. That is why, for Christ's sake, I delight in weaknesses, in insults, in hardships, in persecutions, in difficulties. For when I am weak, then I am strong.

In essence, "For when I am weakened by a thorn, I must lean on and rely on Jesus, and his presence and his perfect love. Then I become strong in his power, not mine."

Weaknesses, insults ... frustrating friends, imperfect spouses, family matters, work, financial, physical and emotional issues – that about covers the thorns list, doesn't it?

God the Father, who loves you perfectly, said to Paul and he says to you: "My grace is sufficient for you, for my power is made perfect in ... *your* ... weakness." (*your* added)

I had operated in my power for years. For years this was all I knew. Everything I had ever learned taught me this was the way, the only way, to operate. What was the alternative? My driving mantra was, "If I don't, it won't. If it's to be, it's up to me!"

That mantra drove me into many a thorn bush. I even carried this approach into 721 Ministries. We started 721 in 2004, and by 2007 I was burning out. Yet back then our schedule was a fraction of what it is today. I was leaning on Sam, and Sam's Self-power, and it was burying me.

But now, because my gracious Father has allowed quite a few thorns to stick in my side, I have learned the alternative: to shove aside Self and live more and more with Jesus' power. Yes, I have learned the secret of living with Holy Spirit power: "I can do all this through him who gives me strength." (Philippians 4:13)

May you learn that in your Self weakness, you can be strong in His strength.

53

9-5 to Eternity

Trust in the Lord with all your heart and lean not on your own understanding; in all your ways submit to him, and he will make your paths straight.

—Proverbs 3:5-6

It was 102 degrees, and the humidity was at 389 percent. I was to meet Gary at his newly purchased house at 4:00 p.m. to quote a renovation job. The house was unoccupied, so it was 140 degrees inside. The clock read 4:15 p.m. but, still, no Gary.

Gary's friend Bob was there, just hanging around I guess. At 4:20, Gary's dad arrived. Gary sauntered in at 4:30. I was not happy. It soon became apparent that they simply were looking for a quote from a contractor to obtain financing for the work that *they* intended to do themselves.

I wanted to express my thoughts, maybe shed a little Sam light into their Neanderthal world. But I decided to ignore my desire to *react* and to instead *respond* properly… maybe shine a little of God's light into their world. Profit: Zero. Two hours wasted. Plus two more spent aggravated.

Three weeks later, the friend Bob called, saying, "I've just left a house with water damage so bad that it's too big for me. These are older folks, and I can't recommend just anyone for the damage repair. I watched you keep your cool earlier this month while my friends were taking advantage of you, and you're the only person I can trust this job to."

Profit: $60,000.00. That was probably the only time that year I responded with the knowledge that I represented Jesus, instead of reacting like I represented Sam... so, no pats on the back, please. And, of course, it's not about receiving monetary rewards from God, but I will say my intent was to fuse my life with Christ into my life at work.

Worship and Work

How do we incorporate our discipleship into our work? How can we keep the light burning in our jobs without running people off with fanatical behavior or ignoring solid business principles? The first question we all have to answer is this: "Is God in the details of life... specifically, in the details of our work?" Be honest about your belief on this.

Let's look at a few governing principles:

- Be effective where you are (1 Cor. 7:17)

- Focus on God and not on your circumstances (Col. 3:23-25)

- Be different (Phil. 2:12-16)

- Plant seeds (1 Cor. 3:5-9)

- Show grace (Col. 4:5-6)

- Keep your focus on *what really matters* (1 Cor. 3:10-15)

I do believe that each of us has been given our own ministry, our own opportunity to shine God's light into this dark world that is hungry—actually, starving—for something more. My wish for you is that you will fuse your worship into your work so that Heaven's welcome committee will say,

Well done, good and faithful servant! You have been faithful with a few things; I will put you in charge of many things. Come and share your master's happiness! (Matt. 25:23)

54

The Gift of Adversity

This particular devotional reading is only intended for a select few, those who have an adversity or two in their lives. If you are perfect, you can stop reading now. If you are already filled to overflowing with the power of the Holy Spirit, disregard this. If your faith and trust in the Lord is already so strong and muscular that you are able to move mountains, take a break as well. But for the rest of us, the few who don't yet have this strong power, let's see how God assures us he will grow us in our faith and our hope—that is, our confident expectation—empowering us with energy, creativity, and clarity... even and especially through the adversities of life.

So, if you have some of them (adversities), read on.

Playing sports in high school in my era rarely involved weightlifting. Maybe one or two of my football teammates lifted weights, but no one on the basketball team and certainly not on my tennis team were weightlifters. (Bunch of wimpy tennis players!)

I had a rude awakening when I got to Clemson and found that everyone on the team was stronger than I was. The starting point guard pushed me around effortlessly. Even the ball boys intimidated me!

So, I got with the strength coach, and he designed a plan to get me stronger, quickly. Let's see... I remember he had me benching about 10 pounds, curling 5, and squatting 15 whole pounds! Boy, was I impressive. After just a few days, I felt like Samson!

Ha! He pushed me relentlessly and challenged me constantly with insidious new ways to torture me. When I would voice my displeasure, he would laugh and say, "But think of this as my gift to you." At times, I was so exhausted and so sore that I felt handicapped by my aching muscles.

But, I got stronger.

The Apostle Paul talked about using the weights of adversity to get stronger. He framed this in a passage that encourages us to cease trying to push through life with our own ego-driven power and learn to rely on the only real power.

So here's the setting. Paul had a "thorn" in his side. It was a major adversity such that he was practically handicapped by it. He complained to God and asked him to take it away. Like us, Paul saw his adversity as an obvious win-lose scenario in which he would "win" if God would take it away but would "lose" if he wouldn't.

Sound familiar? I've had those talks with God. I've presented my recommendations in case God needed some help understanding the situation. But God demurred. He had something better in mind as with Paul:

> ...so I wouldn't get a big head, I was given the gift of a handicap to keep me in constant touch with my limitations. At first I didn't think of it as a gift, and begged God to remove it. Three times I did that, and then he told me, "My grace is enough; it's all you need. My strength and my power become your own in your weakness." (2 Cor. 12:7-9a, MSG)

Paul then reflected on the advantage of God not removing this thorn—that is, he had to rely on God's power without any delusions about his own:

> Once I heard that, I was glad to let it happen. I quit focusing on the handicap and began appreciating the gift. It was a case of Christ's strength moving in on my weakness. Now I take limitations in stride... abuse, accidents, opposition, bad breaks. I just let Christ take

over! And so the weaker I get, the stronger I become. (2 Cor. 12:9b-10, MSG)

It was no longer a win-lose. Paul began to see it as a win-win.

What? I can use adversities to grow in my faith, increasing my muscular trust and growing more powerful within the power of the Holy Spirit? Yes, God can power you up when you see your weaknesses for what they are.

"But I don't want to have to experience pain," I hear you saying. Neither do I. So, let's you and I make a pact: we'll just lift the five-pound weights of avoidance and denial while hoping for the best.

Or, we can acknowledge our fears and our weaknesses—even we macho men have plenty of them—and we can start calling on the power of the Holy Spirit that is already in believers instead of relying on our own five-pound power.

And so, the more I realize my own weaknesses and therefore stop trying to muscle my way through life in my own power, the more I can take a deep breath and call on the power of the Holy Spirit to provide the real heavy lifting.

Imagine that… Through the weightlifting of all my screw-ups, challenges, and adversities, God made me stronger and more energized. And now, I delight in subordinating my ego and my power to God's power, and I am thrilled to see him working above and beyond anything I could have ever pulled off.

55

Nourishing Vs. Maintaining

Jesus promises "life" to us, and he said he meant "life to the full" (John 10:10). He really did mean this, you know. He wants it for you. And you can have it.

But most of us are missing it... all of us are, to varying degrees. Some are missing it badly. You're running on empty, fueled by coffee, busyness, and that next thing that "must" get done.

We are distracted, and we are missing the fullness of life in the Kingdom.

I can just picture Satan reminding his minions at each training session, "Remember, guys, if you can't defeat them, distract them."

Distraction is an old art of war as well as politics... even sports.

I watched Lower Richland High School, coached by Mooney Player, win the South Carolina State Championship game by using distraction. As the teams were lined up and waiting for the opening kickoff, the Lower Richland kicker and his spotter started arguing with each other. They came to blows. Soon, half the kicking team had piled on in a melee. The other team looked on, mesmerized and astonished.

Then, another Lower Richland player stepped over and kicked an onside kick which his teammates easily scooped up and scored. The opponents, totally distracted by the fight, missed the ball entirely.

So do we.

The casualties are our relationships and any hope of intimacy.

Because we are distracted, we tend to try to maintain our relationships instead of nourishing them. We do this with our spouses, our children, our parents, and others who should be important to us. What's the difference? I think you intuitively know. Unfortunately, maintaining a relationship often becomes checking in to check it off your checklist of things that ought to be done. Or must be done.

Maintaining is spending time with someone; *nourishing* is investing time in them.

You know the difference. And trust me... so do they.

We often spend our energy and focus all day on work and activities and fail to invest in our most important relationships. We spend time maintaining but fail to invest time nourishing. Maintaining keeps us in touch while nourishing is when we truly touch.

When you are maintaining, you might be there, but you're not really there. When you are nourishing, you're fully there and in the moment, looking and listening. Remember this: If you're not looking, you're not listening.

Maintaining yields conversations; nourishing yields compassion and caring. You know the difference. Trust me... so do they.

And so does your Heavenly Father.

I'd like you to stop and think for a moment. Are you just maintaining a relationship with Jesus, checking in but typically checked out? Who does all the talking? Come on. Be objective here. Are you truly investing your heart when you are sharing time with the Lord?

Or, are you just phoning it in, multi-tasking with God... maintaining your required religious checklist just to feel safe knowing you're in with God? Ugh. There is no intimacy in maintaining. There is no nourishment. And there is no "life to the full" without both.

Jesus understood that intimacy overflows when we truly give ourselves to him and to each other.

He encourages us,

> Give, and it will be given to you. A good measure,
> pressed down, shaken together and running over, will
> be poured into your lap. For with the measure you use,
> it will be measured to you. (Luke 6:38)

When we nourish, intimacy flourishes.

So may you push back on your distractions, and may you then come to understand God's desire that...

> ...you, being rooted and established in love, may have power, together with all the saints, to grasp how wide and long and high and deep is the love of Christ, and to know this love that surpasses knowledge—that you may be filled to the measure of all the fullness of God. (Eph. 3:18)

"Filled to the measure of all the fullness of God." Intimacy. Nourishment. Life to the full. Overflowing. It takes time. It takes investing. It takes looking and listening... with your loved ones and with your Lord.

56

Trust is the Currency
of Relationship

Why is trust so important to Jesus? You were created to enjoy and thrive in a relationship with him, and he knows that "no trust equals no relationship." Trust is the currency of relationships. And as Josh McDowell so wisely observes, "Rules without relationship equals rebellion."

When a father tells me about his rebellious child—typically, a teenager—and how he plans to squash his or her rebellion with strict, imposing rules, I urge him first to give his child five doses of relationship before ever imposing a rule.

Love on him or her, letting your child know you adore him or her. Take your child to get ice cream. Watch a TV show, movie, or sporting event together. Just have fun—at least, as much as he or she will let you. Create a foundation of loving trust, first, before you start demanding performance. Or, you'll see rebellion—either outwardly or inwardly—which may be worse.

We all intuitively sense the truth in these words: no trust, no true relationship and no true obedience... at least, not obedience from the heart.

My dear little friend, John, whom I adore and love and cherish, gives us the perfect example of an obedient heart... but not out of loving trust. A while back, I took John and his big brother Henry (both under 10 at the time) with me to speak to the local high school football team.

Afterward, we were in the car, talking to my daughter on the speaker phone. I mentioned that her old high school teacher had just rudely interrupted my pre-game talk. Britton said, "Mr. _____ is such a jerk."

After we hung up, John murmured, "One of my teachers is a jerk, too."

Big brother Henry quickly said, "John, we don't say those kinds of words."

To which, precious John replied under his breath in barely a whisper, "I'll say it in my heart if I want to."

"I'll say it in my heart if I want to."

Don't you just love his honest and transparent heart? And yet, is this not a perfect microcosm of us? "I'll obey, outwardly, but only because I have to. Inwardly, in my heart, I'll rebel."

When Jesus said, "Whoever has my commands and obeys them, he is the one who loves me" (John 14:21), he was saying true obedience comes from love. We obey him—or, at least, we are trying to—because we see how much he loves us, not because it's our duty. We see he loved us first, and this engenders our love for him, which bolsters our trust.

Who can love someone robustly and confidently with the full energy and riches of the Kingdom who they cannot trust? Okay, sure, we are called to love unconditionally. Good. Do that. Or try to. But practically speaking, you won't be in a deep, thriving relationship with anyone without trust.

And so it is with your Heavenly Father. Trust is the currency of relationships, with each other and with God.

Imagine the richness of a relationship with your Heavenly Father, with Jesus Christ, saturated with trust and love. You would see God all around you, even and especially in the details of day-to-day living. You would sense his presence and feel his power. Your foundation would be rock solid. You would soar with wings like eagles (Isa. 40:31). Imagine that life. You can have it!

Do you have any issues troubling you right now? Do you have any nagging habits, any sins to which you are a slave? (Yes.) Are you praying to the Lord about them, asking for help?

May I suggest that you stop praying about those specific issues and start asking God to fill you with a growing and strengthening trust in his perfect love? Ask for trust, not answers. Ask for trust, not deliverance. Pray for the power of the Holy Spirit to fill you with trust so that you may be "filled to the measure of all the fullness of God" (Eph. 3:20).

Your nagging habits, sins, and even your scary issues will lose their grip on you as your relationship with the Lord grows deeper, richer, and stronger. You will soar with a new power, fueled by a growing trust.

What a life!

Trust is the currency of relationships.

> He gives strength to the weary and increases the power of the weak. Even youths grow tired and weary, and young men stumble and fall; but those who hope (trust) in the LORD will renew their strength. They will soar on wings like eagles; they will run and not grow weary, they will walk and not be faint. (Isaiah 40:29)

57

Fears or Facts?

"Never will I leave you; never will I forsake you."

—Deuteronomy 31:6

Have you thought much about where fear is disrupting your rhythm in life? Can you see the tentacles of fear that insidiously infect your thoughts and actions, and even more so, your *re-actions*? Fear is rampant in our lives. If you cannot see this, you're just deluding yourself. I, too, resist the idea that fear is controlling my actions, but sadly, fear traps me more than I care to admit.

Jesus had much to say about fear. He is constantly encouraging us not to be afraid, just as he is constantly reassuring us that God is watching, and he cares about the details – your details. He often asked the disciples, "Why are you so afraid?" I can imagine his expression of wonder at their fear, and I can just imagine him thinking, "If you would just listen to me and see that my encouragement is not mere cheerleading, but based in reality – in the facts – there would be no room at the inn for fear in your life."

Try this exercise: Place the following words in the appropriate order of importance to a follower of Jesus: feelings, facts, and faith. Most of us immediately place faith, first. But facts should be first, then faith, with feelings a distant third. You see our faith will waver and wobble, and then our feelings will jump in and take control. But if in these moments we focus on the facts— God is perfect, he is in perfect control, and he loves me perfectly—then our faith is grounded on the rock-solid foundation of the facts, not the slippery and deceiving sand of feelings.

Bette Midler sang out, "God is watching us, God is watching us," and the gospel chorus sways us, lulling us into a warm and fuzzy feeling. But the song title blows it badly. God is not watching us "From a Distance." Jesus' first call to arms is a definitive reassurance that God is here with us, close by, and in control.

> "The time has come," he said. "The kingdom of God is
> near. Repent and believe the good news!"
> (Mark 1:15)

The word for *kingdom* is better translated as *reign*, and *is near* is better translated as *has come*. Jesus is reassuring us that God is here, now, with us, and reigning. The King is not somewhere up in the castle, watching us from a distance, but on the ground and in control.

Now that is good news!

58

Trusting in the Details

When the Babylonian king, Nebuchadnezzar, demanded that Shadrach, Meshach, and Abednego conform to his culture and bow down to his "I am" statue, they said to him,

> "King Nebuchadnezzar, we do not need to defend ourselves before you in this matter. If we are thrown into the blazing furnace, the God we serve is able to deliver us from it, and he will deliver us from Your Majesty's hand. But even if he does not, we want you to know, O King, that we will not serve your gods or worship the image of gold you have set up."
> (Dan. 3:16-18)

Did you catch that? "The God we serve is able to ... he will ... but even if he does not ... we will choose to trust him."

Recently, I had the opportunity to either worry about a situation or relax and leave it in God's hands. I made the choice to relax and leave it in God's hands. Specifically, I should say I chose to leave it in the Holy Spirit's hands. He is the active agent on earth and in our affairs.

I thought through my logic-process as to why I would, and then could, relax and leave it up to the Holy Spirit:

1. I do not know for certain what is the absolute best—in any situation—ever. (If you think you do you are delusional)

But here is what I do know:

2. I know the Holy Spirit is involved in the details.

3. I know God loves me—and the other person in-volved—perfectly. (1 John 4:16-18)

4. I know God is always seeking to conform us to the likeness of Jesus. (Romans 8:29)

5. I know God, because of #4, will always bring good out of every situation. (Romans 8:28)

Based on what I know—and what I know I do not know—why in the world would I want, and then pray for, my way? And why in the world would I not leave it up to the Holy Spirit? As a matter of fact, after working through this logic-process, my actual prayer was, "Do whatever you know is best, Holy Spirit."

How firm are you in the above five statements? Ten percent, forty percent, seventy-five percent?

I am 100 % on #1. No doubt.

I am 100 % on #3-5. No doubt.

I want to say I am 100% on #2, but there is the rub. My feelings rush in and tell me I cannot be 100% certain He is involved in the details—or maybe not in this particular detail. But the facts tell me I can be:

"Are not two sparrows sold for a penny? Yet not one of them will fall to the ground outside your Father's care. And even the very hairs of your head are all numbered. So don't be afraid; you are worth more than many sparrows." (Matt. 10:29-31)

This is Jesus telling us, assuring you and me, that yes indeed, the Father is deeply aware of and deeply involved in your details.

The next time anxiety and worry come knocking on your heart, may you remind yourself of these facts, and choose to close the door to those feelings-imposters.

It really will be simply your choice: Jesus' facts or your feelings.

59

The Coronavirus:
Lie Down—Slow Down

He makes me lie down in green pastures, he leads me beside quiet waters, he refreshes my soul.

—Psalm 23:2-3

This morning I was chatting with my dear friend Patrick

about the sudden halt to all our normal activities. Patrick has five children, all in the midst of school activities, sports, swimming, dance, and friends – you name it, they are involved in it. Even though my friend leads a fairly balanced life, and his focus is on what is truly important, with five children he unavoidably has many, many moving parts.

I am sure you can relate. The response I so often get from someone when I ask how they are doing is, "We are wide open!" I have heard this so many times when inviting someone to be a part of a study: "Well, soccer is ramping up and travel baseball, too. My wife will be going one direction each weekend and I will be going another. I don't see any way we can get involved."

Oh my.

In the midst of this "forced slowdown" Psalm 23 leaps to mind:

The Lord is my shepherd, I lack nothing.
He makes me lie down in green pastures, he leads me
     beside quiet waters, he refreshes my soul. He
     guides me along the right paths for his name's sake.
Even though I walk through the darkest valley, I will
     fear no evil, for you are with me; your rod and your
     staff, they comfort me.
You prepare a table before me in the presence of my
     enemies. You anoint my head with oil; my cup
     overflows.
Surely your goodness and love will follow me all the
     days of my life, and I will dwell in the house of the
     Lord forever. (Psalm 23)

I hope this Psalm is a comfort to you during these stressful and uncertain times. Yes, I do. But may I ask you to focus on one aspect of this message?

He makes me lie down in green pastures, he leads me
     beside quiet waters, he refreshes my soul.

Might God be looking for you to use this time to ... slow down? Might He wish to see you take a deep breath, relax and focus on the only thing that is truly important in life:
Relationships.
Relationship with Jesus.
Relationship with your loved ones.
Whether or not God allowed this virus to go pandemic so we would all slow down, I can assure you He is now looking to see how you handle this time. He wants you to slow down. If you refuse, He will make you.
The Holy Spirit through David states the case plainly:

He ... makes me lie down ... he leads me beside still
     waters.

The message is clear: God will first lead you to still waters. But if you insist on staying wide open, He will lovingly make you lie down.

May you use this time to learn again how to lie down. May you seek still waters for your soul. And may you use this time to go deeper in your relationship with Jesus.

And finally, may you be refreshed in this time when you simply cannot be "wide open."

60

Worrying About Hurrying

1. Are you worried; are you hurried?
2. What are you learning; what are you changing?
3. What will be your story after this?

I have been asking the men these three questions since the coronavirus stopped us all in our tracks. Today we will consider 1 and 2.

By now most of us have been forced to stop hurrying, because there is nothing to hurry to. What a 'plate-tectonics shift" that has been for so many people.

Nothing to hurry to! (No emails please on the grammar)

Nothing to hurry to. What a radical way to live. But of course, it is simply naive and silly to even ponder this in our culture today. "Don't be silly. We must keep moving. Hurrying is a part of life. The children must stay busy!"

So, are you learning anything – about your life? Are you seeing things differently now? Perhaps a new sense of clarity – about what is truly important? If so, then you will be changing things.

That is, unless you are stupid, and go right back to the hurried and worried life you were living before this C-19 shutdown.

Worrying Because I Am Hurrying

Is this not the most asinine way to live? The insanity of setting up a schedule – for me, for my family – that causes us … forces us … *to have to hurry* from one thing to the next? Can there be a more foolish, self-inflicted illness?

Perhaps the most important thing we can take into our post C-19 life is this simple fact:

Saying yes means saying no.

When you say yes to anything – any activity – then you will be forced to say no to something else. That's the fact, Jack! For most of us we blindly say yes to eternally insignificant things, and therefore unwittingly say no to eternally significant things.

We say yes to TV, social media, committees and activities of all sorts. Some of these are good things, but they force us to say no to the best things – such things as relationships, time with our loved ones, meals at home together, exercise, rest, sleep, quieter times of reflection.

Time with our Lord.

Remember Dallas Willard's stinging observation:

If what you are doing is not eternally significant, then
it is eternally insignificant.

We all have been forced to slow down, but I like to think about it like this: Our loving Heavenly Father stepped in and said his own "No" to all our insignificant, hurrying around activities. He did this because he knew we had been blinded by the culture, and could not even see the madness of our hurrying around life.

Now he wants you to stay tuned in to his message. And to carry it forward.

May you learn to declare "No!" to all those eternally insignificant activities, so you can say a resounding "Yes!" to the most important things in life.

61

Confusion to Order

Logos, (Greek: "word," "reason," or "plan") in Greek phi-losophy and theology, the divine reason implicit in the cosmos, ordering it and giving it form and meaning.

Have you spent any time digging into the Prologue at the beginning of the Gospel of John? Please do. It is mesmerizing in its lofty prose and its beautiful flow. I have been captivated by John's opening words in verses 1-18 since I was born again in 1995.

I think you will, too—if you will take the time to drink it in. May I suggest you first gulp all eighteen verses down a couple of times, and then go back and sip them one verse at a time?

John opens with a declaration that has both captured and confused many for eons:

> In the beginning was the Word ... the Logos, and the Word ... the Logos was with God, and the Word ... the Logos was God.

John is writing in Greek, identifying Jesus as the Logos. He does this for a specific reason. John is living in Ephesus when he writes his Gospel. Ephesus is the "Jewel of Asia" —a fabulous port city thriving with commerce, as well as medical practice and research. But more importantly for John's purpose, Ephesus is a major center for philosophical debate in the Greco-Roman world.

So what?

Around the year 500 B.C. a famous philosopher named Heraclitus stood beside a river and made this famous observation: "No man can step in the same river twice. For he is not the same man, and it is not the same river."

Heraclitus was perplexed by the ever-changing nature of the world around him, and posed the question, "How can there be any order or design to such a changing world?"

His answer? The Logos: The reason, the supreme logic that created the world. The principle that orders the world.

Around 400 B.C. Plato, after debating and discussing this Logos for decades, concluded this: "It may be that someday there will come forth from God a word, a Logos, that will reveal all mysteries and make everything plain."

Around 90 A.D. John, in a stroke of pure—Holy Spirit-inspired—genius, captures this mystery the Greeks and Romans, and even the Jews, have been debating for centuries in his opening words:

> In the beginning, this power, this force that you all say brings order and form to this universe; this Logos, who you hope may perhaps one day come from God so we can understand what He is doing in this world? Well, he came. He lived among us. He taught, he performed miracles, and he sacrificed his life for us.
> This mystery you have been contemplating for all these centuries?
> His name is Jesus."

Do you want to know where Heraclitus was living when he first introduced this Logos to the philosophical world? Ephesus. Just like John. 500 B.C. to 90 A.D.

No coincidences.

John wanted the Greco-Roman world to know Jesus is it ... the one who came and made sense of all their confusion. But more importantly he wants you to know Jesus is the one who can make sense of the confusion in your life.

He will bring order and reason to the ever-changing, white water rapids of this cultural chaos in which we live. He won't necessarily change the world around you, but he will change the world within you. That is his guarantee.

Confusion to order. Change to consistency. Perplexed to peace.

62

Tohu wa-bohu to Tov

John begins his Gospel, "In the beginning," to take us back to Genesis 1 and the creation story. Here is God's own the description of the universe prior to creation.

> In the beginning God created the heavens and the earth. Now the earth was formless and empty, darkness was over the surface of the deep, and the Spirit of God was hovering over the waters. (Gen. 1:1-2)

Formless and empty, darkness and void. This is all captured in the Hebrew expression tohu wa-bohu, and it carries with it a sense of chaos, as well. What a wonderful word phrase. Tohu wa-bohu. In the beginning there seemed to be no order, no purpose, no logic, no ... Logos. But then God said, "Let there be light," and the show was on!

God then began to create spaces and fill those spaces. The voids filled. The darkness became light. The disorder ordered. The formless formed. And as God said, "It was tov ... it was good."

In the beginning of my life there was much tohu wa-bohu. I was blind and didn't know it. I was stumbling around in the darkness, like the people Isaiah describes:

> The people walking in darkness have seen a great light;
> on those living in the land of deep darkness a light has
> dawned. (Isa. 9:2)

But then God said, "Let there be light in Sam's life." And the light came on. The formless started to form. The disorder started to find order. The tohu wa-bohu became tov.

It was good. And, oh boy, his tov has just gotten better and better.

I had been living with inner chaos in my life all along, but I was so blinded by this vapid culture, I couldn't see the chaos. It felt normal—like everyone else around me. I didn't know what I didn't know.

Before the Light came on, I had tried everything under the sun to dampen down the inner chaos, but of course I was looking for tov in all the wrong places: sports, work, "sex, drugs and rock & roll." You name it, I tried it. But the tohu wa-bohu swirled on. The tov I was so desperately seeking was beyond my grasp.

Yes, the Spirit was hovering over the chaotic waters of my life, but I was under water and didn't know who the Spirit was. Then God said, "Enough! Let there be light." And the light came on.

Perhaps you can identify with this inner chaos, this darkness, and these voids? Or you may be one who has successfully avoided the chaos without Jesus. I doubt it. You may think you have, but when the light comes on, you will know his tov has alluded you.

How do you leave the tohu wa-bohu behind and find his tov? You surrender. You surrender "my claim to my right to myself,"[1] and you start to follow Jesus, who beckons to you even now, saying,

> "I am the light of the world. Whoever follows me will never walk in darkness, but will have the light of life." (John 8:12)

---

[1] Oswald Chambers

63

Amazing Peace

When Jesus heard this [from the Centurion], he was amazed at him, and turning to the crowd following him, he said, "I tell you, I have not found such great trust even in Israel."

—Luke 7:9

Being in a men's ministry, I often am witness to some very messy situations. I have the privilege to witness some men face these trials with confidence in their Father – anxious, yes, but they refuse to be overwhelmed with fear.

The Centurion and these friends face extreme circumstances in which they display extreme trust. Maybe you'll be "lucky" enough not to be faced with such difficulty, but you can display this rock-solid trust even in the details of your everyday life, and it will be just as pleasing to God the Father.

We are all presented with an array of opportunities to trust, or instead to fear and worry. Little annoyances that don't go our way. Bigger frustrations that upset our little worlds. Some very real. Some blown way out of proportion.

When the contract is delayed or even cancelled. When that repair bill is much higher than expected. When your husband or wife is not acting right. Or when your child is wandering.

Maybe it's just that my incessant need for immediate gratification has been delayed.

Or, perhaps you just can't see God moving and just can't feel his presence. In these situations you can choose to react in fear or respond in faith...to worry or to trust. One is a path to peace; the other is an avenue to anxiety.

And even when you just *try* to trust, Jesus embraces your feeble attempts, just as he did with the distressed dad whose possessed son was flailing around in the fire.

When Jesus told the father, "I can do anything if you will just trust me," he cried out, as I so often do, "I believe; help me with my unbelief!" Even this mere *attempt* to trust obviously amazed Jesus, and he responded immediately (Mark 9:24).

In extreme trials and challenges, and even in day-to-day irritations and problems, amazing an amazing Jesus with an unwavering trust leads to the peace that surpasses all understanding.

Start today. Right now. Wherever you are. Whatever you are facing, big or small...and say, "I'm ready to start trusting you, Jesus. But I need your help."

Then get ready, because he will amaze you.

64

The Weight of Wait

It is a few days before Pentecost and the disciples are in Jerusalem. Jesus was crucified and resurrected around forty days prior. Since then they have seen him many times, and most recently up in Galilee. There he had breakfast on the beach with them (John 21 – a truly lovely story) and also appeared to them, along with five hundred of their closest friends, to give them the "Great Commission" (Matthew 28).

Now they are back in Jerusalem for the Feast of Shavuot/Pentecost, because this is one of the three annual feasts to which the Jews are required to travel to the Holy City. (My apologies to Charleston)

Remember, Pentecost is the Greek name for the Old Testament Hebrew name Shavuot. Shavuot celebrates the giving of the Torah at Mt. Sinai. We celebrate Pentecost, the giving of the Holy Spirit at Mt. Moriah—the Temple Mount.

Dr. Luke picks up the story here:

> On one occasion, while he was eating with them, he gave them this command: "Do not leave Jerusalem, but wait for the gift my Father promised ..." Acts 1:4 (The promised gift is the promised Holy Spirit.)

Now please notice Jesus was very specific: "but wait for the Holy Spirit."

I can just see Jesus looking at Peter, impetuous, cannot sit still, Peter, and emphasizing the word "wait." Jesus knows the heart of the disciples, and he knows yours, too. He knows we do not like to wait. We like action. We like motion. Motion and action satisfy our, "If I don't, it won't," inner nervousness. Motion and action pacify our, "If it's to be, it's up to me," compulsion.

But Jesus knows the disciples could not possibly know the next right thing to do, until the Holy Spirit shows them. And before Pentecost the disciples did not yet have the Holy Spirit. He knew they – or at least their leader Peter – would feel like they had to do something. They couldn't just sit around and pray, and wait for the Holy Spirit's guidance.

So, Jesus stated emphatically, "Wait."

A good friend recently related a story from his Harvard MBA days. His professor was discussing decision making. He drew a "decision tree" on the board, and discussed how to lay out all the available options, in order to solve a difficult problem. Then the professor said this:

"Of all the students I have had over all these years, rarely does anyone remember what I am about to tell you. There is another option that is not on your decision tree. This option carries equal weight, if not an even greater weight, than all these other action-options you have listed."

The professor paused, surveyed the students, and then said, "And that is the option to wait, to do nothing."

Argh!

I do not like to wait. I like to move ahead. I like to make decisions, and then carry them out. Action! Motion!

Why do I not like to wait? Because I might not get my way. Things may not go as I know they must. Only patsies wait. Real men take action.

If I wait on the Holy Spirit, he may want to do it another way. He may even want to do it a way that I do not like. Oh sure, if I am sitting in Sunday School, I am going to parrot the party line: "Of course I want what God wants. His will not mine," and all that.

But in my human heart I want my way – because it is, I am sure, the best way.

Ugh.

What about you?

65

Casting Lots

Be still, and know that I am God.

—Ps. 46:10

Previously we saw that Peter and the boys just could not follow Jesus' very specific instructions to wait – to wait until the Holy Spirit came to them on Pentecost. Jesus knew they could not possibly know the next right thing to do without the Spirit's clarity and guidance.

And neither can you.

He also knew Peter and the boys were not inclined to wait. This, "I must take action," this, "I must make a decision and act on it ... now!" trait is all too human, and has led to so many bad decisions and untimely, unnecessary, and unhelpful actions.

Can I get an "Amen?"

Blaise Pascal, the French mathematician and philosopher, the man credited with the origins of calculus, said this:

> All men's miseries derive from not being able to sit in a quiet room alone.

Perhaps a bit of hyperbole, but perhaps not by much.

So, what happens next? Peter takes action. First, he stands up and quotes scripture. This is always a bit dicey when one is quoting scripture without the same Spirit who wrote the scriptures. Actually, he misquotes scripture.

And based on his misquoting of scripture he says this:

> "Therefore it is necessary to choose one of the men who have been with us the whole time the Lord Jesus was living among us, beginning from John's baptism to the time when Jesus was taken up from us. For one of these must become a witness with us of his resurrection." (Acts 1:21-22)

Do you see the action imperative words here: "necessary" – "must"? I think it would have been helpful if someone in the room would have said, "Peter, why is it *necessary* ... why *must* we ...? Should we perhaps do what Jesus said, and wait?"

Now look what happens next. This is so classic. I have no doubt I have done this several times over the years. They formulated a plan, put the plan in motion, and then asked God to bless their plan.

> So **they** nominated two men ... **Then they prayed**, "Lord, you know everyone's heart. Show us which of these two you have chosen to take over this apostolic ministry, which Judas left to go where he belongs." (Acts 1:23-25, bold added)

"They nominated," and then they prayed. Not, "They prayed and then they nominated." No sir. They nominated – and then they asked the Lord to bless their plans.

Have you ever done this? Of course you have. Have your church leaders ever done this? You bet they have.

I have a plan. I like my plan. So I put my plan in action. And then, perhaps to curry a little holy insurance, I pause to pray. I do not wait for an answer, mind you, because I already have my plan. I am not actually looking for an answer; I am looking for God to cooperate.

And to really add insult to injury, look what the disciples did next:

> Then they cast lots, and the lot fell to Matthias; so he was added to the eleven apostles. (Acts 1:26)

They cast lots. Jesus' dedicated followers cast lots. They rolled the dice. Do you think they learned this from Jesus? I have read the gospels many times, and I have yet to find Jesus playing dice games to discern God's will.

But when one is executing one's own plan, with no guidance or clarity from the Holy Spirit, one might as well roll the dice. Or consult the tea leaves, or that month's horoscope.

My friends, please learn to wait, to ask the Holy Spirit for guidance. I promise you, actually Jesus promises you, it is safe to wait. I can assure you the Holy Spirit will help clarify your situations, and he will provide guidance for you, if you want him to.

And if you want him to, you must be willing to wait. Maybe only for a few seconds, or minutes, or hours, or days – more likely days – but please, please learn to be still.

66

Repent & Come Home

He was born in the summer of his 27th year
Coming home to a place he'd never been before*
He left yesterday behind him, you might say he was
born again
You might say he found a key for every door

—"Rocky Mountain High"

Imagine we are standing with the huge crowd that has gathered around Peter and the disciples on the day of Pentecost. We are at the Temple Mount. The Holy Spirit has come in full force with fire and wind, rumbling and lots of commotion.

Three thousand-plus of us have gathered around, and we are all hearing the disciples speaking in our own native tongues. What a sight to behold! Peter stands up and gives a doozy of a sermon, and as he finishes:

> When the people heard this, they were cut to the heart and said to Peter and the other apostles, "Brothers, what shall we do?"
>
> Peter replied, "Repent and be baptized, every one of you, in the name of Jesus Christ for the forgiveness

of your sins. And you will receive the gift of the Holy Spirit." (Acts 2:37-38)

"They were cut to the heart." This seems an appropriate response when one hears the truth of the gospel. "Cut to the heart" shows you did not just hear the words, but the truth penetrated your heart. Your otherwise comfort-seeking, lukewarm heart was assaulted, and conviction stirs you to respond as the people did:

"Brothers, what shall we do?"

I want you to notice what Peter does not say in response to their question. He does not say, "Do something. Do anything. Just get busy working for God!"

No, he says, "Repent."

Repent? As in: Say I am sorry for my bad habits and sinful actions, and then try to stop doing them?

Well, yes, but that is a very limited idea of repenting.

Repentance means to change direction, but with a strong undercurrent of coming … Home. Coming Home to Jesus. Coming Home to your Heavenly Father. Coming Home perhaps to a place you have never been before.* Repentance means getting off your current path and getting on God's path.

There are only two paths in life: God's path and all the other paths. Only one path leads Home. God's path is a Holy Spirit led path. All the other paths can be distilled into either Self's path or the Culture-led path.

The path on which I typically find myself when I have drifted from God's path is either my Self's path or the culture-led path. Both of which have led me into a ditch on too many occasions to count.

How to know if you are off God's path? Ask yourself this excellent question:

> Is where you are going where you want to be when you get there? (Andy Stanley)

How to know what path to choose?
This is what the Lord says:

Stand at the crossroads and look; ask for the ancient
   paths,
ask where the good way is, and walk in it, and you
   will find rest for your souls. (Jeremiah 6:16)

Is that not beautiful? Please read it again and let it soak through into your soul.

Because yes, God's path will lead to rest for your souls.

I will finish with C.S. Lewis' observation on repenting:

Now what was the sort of 'hole' man had got himself into? He had tried to set up on his own, to behave as if he belonged to himself. In other words, fallen man is not simply an imperfect creature who needs improvement:

He is a rebel who must lay down his arms.

Laying down your arms, surrendering, saying you're sorry, realizing that you have been on the wrong track and getting ready to start life over again from the ground floor – that is the only way out of our 'hole.' This process of surrender … is what Christians call repentance. (CS Lewis, *Mere Christianity*)

Part 4

Perspective

67

The Name Jesus

Therefore God exalted him to the highest place and gave him the name that is above every name, that at the name of Jesus every knee should bow, in heaven and on earth and under the earth, and every tongue acknowledge that Jesus Christ is Lord, to the glory of God the Father.

—Philippians 2:9-11

I have a New Year's proposition for you. Not a resolution; let's call it a January challenge. For the next three weeks I want you to say the name "Jesus" each time you get ready to say "God." I have been practicing this for a few months now, and I am still getting used to it.

Why would I suggest this? It is clear from the New Testament scriptures that God the Father's plan all along is for Jesus the Son to be the catalyst in any relationship with him. A cursory reading of the NT unequivocally affirms this:

> In the beginning was the Word (Jesus) ...Through him all things were made; without him nothing was made that has been made. In him was life, and that life was the light of all mankind. (John 1:1-4)

The Son is the image of the invisible God, the firstborn over all creation. For in him all things were created: things in heaven and on earth ... all things have been created through him and for him. He is before all things, and in him all things hold together. And he is the head of the body, the church; he is the beginning and the firstborn from among the dead, so that in everything he might have the supremacy. (Colossians 1:15-18)

Yes, Jesus is the catalyst.

Please hear me on this: I am not trying in any way to introduce some new theology here. And I am certainly not intruding on the majesty of the Trinity. It is a simple exercise designed to draw you closer to Jesus.

If you want to go deeper in your relationship with Jesus, say his name. Jesus told his disciples during his last supper with them that they were his friends – not just his disciples. So yes, Jesus is my Savior, and more and more he has become Lord of my life. He is my rabbi and yes, he is God Almighty!

But he is also my best friend and my closet confident. So I say his name – often.

The name God can be a bit vague and ambiguous. But not Jesus. Jesus walked around with us. He talked and ate and slept, and even wept with us. He is tangible. His name evokes a visceral response.

Here is what you will find if you accept this friendly proposal. It will be a challenge. It can be awkward. It can even be a bit embarrassing. It will certainly not come naturally, and this is why I have found this exercise to be so valuable.

It creates an awareness of Jesus in my mind that is not as prevalent if I am typically saying the name God. Jesus becomes more personal, more present, and more pervasive throughout my walking and talking day.

And that is a good thing.

In the South, especially, one can say the name God at parties and not feel awkward. Perhaps even around the country one can say God in a social setting and not be ostracized. But try saying Jesus and see what happens. The air will go out of the conversation and you will see an immediate "stiffening up." Even among professing Christians.

Try it. I can assure you that you will stumble at first. But as the name Jesus becomes more natural to you, so will his friendship. As his friendship becomes more personal, so will the richness and the sweetness of your spiritual life with Jesus.

Jesus is the catalyst. If you want to get closer to him, and trust me you do, say his name. So for the rest of this month say Jesus every time. You will be shocked how clumsy it feels, but how valuable it becomes.

P.S.

And by the way, because Jesus is my best friend I call him by his name – not his title. "Christ" is Jesus' title, not his name. The proper way to say "Christ" is to say "the Christ," as it is the Greek word for Messiah. It is my observation that people who call Jesus, "Christ," often do not know him on a first-name basis. If that stings, or even offends, perhaps – how can I say this gently and politely? – it should.

68

Busyness

Satan's number one weapon is busyness. I have witnessed many a soul lost to Satan through busyness. And because of busyness I have also witnessed many a man or woman find salvation, but miss the Life to the Full Jesus promised. As the Way has grown and spread, our slower and more meditative Hebrew culture has mixed and assimilated with the other cultures of the world. The busier cultures of the larger cities have promulgated this weapon of Satan quickly.

The Holy Spirit brings peace, and clarity, and, remember: God is a God of order, not distraction.

I see men and women scurrying around all week trying to get it all done. I see these same folks scurrying around on our days of worship trying to get all their worship activities done. During the week they are busy with work and activities. And even though most of our Believers honor the Lord's Day by not working at their jobs, they still busy themselves with church 'activities' on the Lord's Day.

They are missing the one thing that is most important: knowing Jesus. It is much easier to work for God than to know God. The truth is many people would rather serve God than get to know him personally and intimately. Perhaps this is because serving God is tangible, and therefore measurable, and so this is where they find their reward.

Serving God for our sense of activity and accomplishment bears no fruit ... that will last.

I am reminded of the Psalm:

Unless the Lord builds the house, the builders labor in
 vain.
Unless the Lord watches over the city, the guards
 stand watch in vain.
In vain you rise early and stay up late, toiling for food
 to eat—
for he grants sleep to those he loves.

I know many men – and a few Martha's too – who rise early
and stay up late, and lose much sleep because of their, "If I don't, it
won't," mindset. But when we are building with the Lord, and
through the power of the Spirit, peaceful sleep comes naturally.

Because we have abandoned the outcome to Jesus.

Busyness mistakes motion for movement. People imprisoned
by busyness have much motion in their lives, but they are not moving closer to Jesus.

A tragic life is the life that seeks things that are measurable in
the moment, instead of things that are measurable eternally. I have
found that things that are measurable in the short term are neither
measurable nor memorable in the long term.

69

Busy Martha

You may remember Jesus' dear friends, Lazarus, Martha
and Mary. Jesus loved all three equally, but he seemed to truly relish
his time with Lazarus, the older brother. I think he felt like he could
just sit and be himself with Lazarus. Lazarus' home was quiet, and
the two of them would sit all afternoon just talking about the scriptures and the Father.

Lazarus asked a lot of deep questions, many I would never
have even thought of. And Jesus really enjoyed asking Lazarus challenging questions in return. This kind of give and take debate gave
Jesus great joy.

Their conversations, and sometimes debates, could go on for
hours. The younger sister Mary would sit near them and listen to all
they said, absorbing their words deep into her heart. She had such
a peaceful way about her. Neither she nor Lazarus ever seemed to
be in a hurry, and Mary would not let anything distract her from
listening intently to Jesus.

But Martha was just the opposite of Mary. Don't get me wrong,
she was a pleasant person, and friendly and welcoming. She loved
to have Jesus visit, and would always prepare great meals for us.
The twelve of us loved it when Jesus said we were stopping in Beth-
any!

But Martha could be difficult. She would get distracted by all
the preparations that had to be made. I remember the time she
worked herself into a frenzy, cleaning the house and getting the
food ready. When she got into this mode I would be sure to stay out

of her way. I had been bossed around by Martha before, and even snapped at when I didn't do something the way she wanted it done.

I have no doubt Martha considered Mary lazy. And she certainly thought of her as inefficient, and surely a time-waster. Martha reminded me of ... me, back in my fishing days. Rushed, hurried and harried, temper rising and patience falling.

I was watching her get worked up, and I elbowed John in the side and said, "Watch out. Martha is getting frustrated." John looked her way and saw her face reddening, and quietly walked outside. So did Nathaniel and Philip.   They knew better than to get in the way of Martha when she was pressing and stressing.

I watched her finally drop her spoon and march over to Jesus and Lazarus. She came to Jesus and cried out, "Lord, don't you care that my sister has left me to do the work by myself? Tell her to help me!"

I have to say I was trying my best to suppress a smile. Poor Martha. She was, after all, doing all the work. She was hot, and she was weary, and she was tired. But the thing is she actually liked being this way. She thrived on being busy. Some of us had tried before to help her and she pushed us out of the way, murmuring, "If you want something done right, you have to do it yourself."

Can you relate?

70

"Good" Distractions: Keeping Sight of Your Priorities

I have written several Putting Greens on the topic of *busyness.* I tried to make you see that the Villain (Satan) uses busyness as his #1 weapon against you. And the victims of this assault are our relationships—with the Lord and with each other—as well as our bodies, minds, and spirits.

But I admit defeat. Busyness has too strong a hold on our society… and on you. The battle there is lost. Most of you dismissed me out of hand. The ones who accepted my premise eventually shrugged, "You are right, but I cannot do anything about it. The tide is too strong. The die is cast."

So, today, I've switched my focus from *busyness* to *distractions.*

I am often approached by men who say some variation on this theme: "I've been meaning to get to the 721 men's lunches, but something keeps coming up." Or, "I really want to come, but you know how it is… If a client calls and wants to meet, I have to."

I wonder what these men would say if they already had another client scheduled when that call came… or, if "something came up." Would they cancel the existing appointment? Don't be silly. But, of course, the idea of scheduling in advance a firm time with God—at a 721 meeting or wherever—is simply ludicrous; isn't it?

And if they were so foolish and naïve as actually to make a meeting time with God a fixed commitment in their schedule—say, before the busy week begins—they would have abandoned all reason and flung themselves on the chopping block of society. Certainly, no one can rely on God to honor this kind of misguided trust.

Your "yes" is so often to something good but nowhere near to the best. And your "no", then—unintentionally but unavoidably—must be to the best.

Being distracted by good opportunities will cause you to miss the very best. And Jesus tells story after story about distractions causing us to miss him and his Kingdom. The third soil in the Parable of the Four Soils is a prime example:

The seed that fell among thorns stands for those who hear, but as they go on their way they are choked by life's worries, riches and pleasures... (Luke 8:14)

So, I ask you to sit down for a moment—can you?—and write down what the absolute most important things are to you. Hopefully, time with your Lord, your spouse, and your children will be at the top... followed perhaps by exercise, rest, relaxation, sleep, walks... dare I say, even naps?

Take your Daytimer, online calendar, or an index card and schedule them in each week. Immovable, unchangeable... priorities.

Now, with your best priorities fixed in place, consider all future opportunities and invitations as potential enemies to the best.

The next time you are approached about serving on a committee, chairing a board, or signing your child up for yet another activity, respond, "I'll have to weigh this against my *best* priorities, and then I'll have to determine what I'd have to say 'no' to."

Your old way of responding is to say "yes" mindlessly without thinking about the consequences of saying "no" to the best.

But now, because you've already scheduled in your exercise, a walk with your spouse, play time with your daughter, or personal time with the Lord, you examine your schedule for openings, first. First!

If you decide this new opportunity or invitation is important enough to say "no" to something you've already committed to as part of the best, what then will you say "no" to? Because, make no mistake, you now will have to say "no" to something.

No openings? "No, I couldn't possibly do it" is the correct reply.

And saying "no" to yourself and your body-mind-spirit needs is just as damaging if not more so.

Jesus warned us over and over that it would be the good distractions that would cause us to miss him, his Kingdom, and his Kingdom living.

Don't be a distracted, good Fool, and miss his best.

You may be saying, "What if everybody took this approach? Nothing would ever get done."

To which I would say, "If everyone did this, we'd get a lot more of the important... the best... things done. We'd live in a much saner world with the divorce rate cut in half and burnout and exhaustion mitigated. Stressed out children would be a thing of the past, and children growing up with the devoted attention from their... relaxed... parents would be the norm."

The best?

71

Superman: X-Ray Vision

The people walking in darkness
   have seen a great light;
on those living in the land of deep darkness
   a light has dawned.

—Isaiah 9:2

Do you remember when the Christopher Reeves' *Superman* movie came out back in 1978? A group of us boys went to see the movie and were blown away by the special effects. At one point Superman is flying through the sky, and he casually drops his left shoulder and eases off to the left in this intercontinental super swoop. It was so cool.

One Halloween I dressed up as Superman, and boy was I on top of the world. I was ready to conquer all the bad guys, until that flimsy band on my mask broke about five minutes into the night. And then the cape wouldn't stay on, much less flow behind me, as I acted like I was flying by running at breakneck speed.

Which of Superman's powers would you most like to have? I think it is still fun to think about: the ability to fly, super strength, super hearing, x-ray vision, or reading minds?

When I was younger, I would have automatically said flying. Soaring around in the sky – how great would that be? And of course having super strength would have been really cool with the girls. But as I season through life, I more and more recognize the extraordinary value in being able to see things ... clearly and accurately. So for me it's now x-ray vision, but in the sense of Holy Spirit discernment, clarity and spiritual vision.

Do you think you can see things clearly? Don't kid yourself. I used to think so. When I was younger, I had it all figured out. Now, though, I'm not so self-assured. I now realize my natural vision is clouded. It is clouded with prejudice, with bias, with pre-conceived notions, negative assumptions, and don't miss this: powerful self-serving strongholds.

But my ability to see with clarity is hindered mostly by my myopic perspective, clouded with Self.

But ... the more I seek to see through the Light of Jesus' perspective on life, the more I begin to truly *see*. Jesus tried to tell me this a long time ago:

> "I am the light of the world. Whoever follows me will
> never walk in darkness, but will have the light of life."
> (John 8:12)

And so did Van Morrison, a couple thousand years later:

> Whenever God, shines his light on me,
> Opens up my eyes, so I can see"
> (From the song "Whenever God Shines His Light On
> Me")

72

Apart from Your Performance

However, each one of you also must love his wife as he loves himself, and the wife must respect her husband.

—Eph. 5:33

When I am officiating a wedding, one of my go-to passages is this one from Ephesians. Of course, I discuss this extensively with the bride and groom during pre-marital counseling because, who are we kidding, they won't remember much of what I say during the ceremony itself. Did you?

During our pre-marital discussions, my main point is this: Husbands, in that moment of frustration, or disappointment, or even anger, please remember your wife needs your unconditional love first and foremost—apart from her performance ... especially in your eyes.

Wives, in those same moments, your husband needs your unconditional respect—apart from his performance ... again, especially in your eyes.

Can I get an "Amen?"

Of course, the wife needs respect and the husband needs love, too. But God the Father knows how we are each designed, and so of course he knows our primary needs.**

But my point today is more about "apart from his or her performance ... in your eyes."

Is this not what we are all searching for ... to be seen in a light most favorable, even when we mess up? You want your spouse to love you and respect you, and you want them to do so apart from your performance. We all do. Our hearts deeply yearn for this.

I add "in your eyes" because our spouse's eyes are what matter most to us in that moment of conflict. That "look" can indeed kill the spirit in our hearts.

But your Heavenly Father's eyes see you apart from your performance. Even when you do not deserve it. My performance typically lacks luster, certainly in the eyes of a perfect God. But I can rest in the assurance of his love for me, and his promise to always be with me, even until the end of the age, is not conditional on my performance.

What a monumental relief. With this promise I can rest, and you can rest, from performance mode, and find peace in pleasing our Father. Pleasing, not performance. Joy power not will power. Blessings not burdens.

(Remember though, I am not going soft on obedience: obeying God is essential to the life that is truly life. But I am going hard against judging eyes.)

Jesus says:

> If your eyes are good, your whole body will be full of
> light. But if your eyes are bad, your whole body will be
> full of darkness. (Matt. 6:22-23)

A better reading is this: "When your eyes are generous, your whole body will be full of light. But if your eyes are stingy and judgmental, your whole body will be full of darkness."

If you want to live in the flow of the Kingdom among us, you will first receive this promise, that your Father views you with generous eyes, apart from your performance. And as you start to live with this promise, you will then seek to view your spouse, your children, indeed everyone, in a light most favorable, with bright and generous eyes—apart from their performance.

73

Pride: Posing and Posturing

I have spoken about remembering God in all my ways.
God reminds us to remember Him throughout His scriptures. Here is a familiar reminder:

> Trust in the LORD with all your heart, and lean not on your own understanding. In all your ways acknowledge him, and he will make your paths straight. (Prov. 3:5-6)

When I remind myself to acknowledge Him, in essence to see Him in all the details, then I will not so easily drift into seeing Sam in all the details. Thus pride is dammed up, and humility flows from within. C.S. Lewis captures this perfectly:

> We must not think pride is something God forbids because he is offended at it, or that humility is something he demands as due to his own dignity—as if God himself was proud. He is not in the least worried about his dignity.
>
> The point is, he wants you to know him: wants to give you himself. And he and you are two things of such a kind that if you really get into any kind of touch with him you will, in fact, be humble—delightfully humble, feeling the infinite relief of having for once got

rid of all the silly nonsense about your own dignity which has made you restless and unhappy all your life.

He is trying to make you humble in order to make this moment possible: trying to take off a lot of silly, ugly, fancy-dress in which we have all got ourselves up and are strutting about like the little idiots we are.

I wish I had got a bit further with humility myself: if I had, I could probably tell you more about the relief, the comfort, of taking the fancy-dress off—getting rid of the false self, with all its 'Look at me' and 'Aren't I a good boy?' and all its posing and posturing. To get even near it, even for a moment, is like a drink of cold water to a man in a desert. (excerpt from *Mere Christianity*)

I hate all the posing and posturing, don't you? I lived this way for a long time, and the immense relief C.S. Lewis refers to is so joyful and so relaxing. But if I do not continually remind myself that I live in a God-saturated world, I will drift back into a Sam-saturated world, and I will again find myself a slave to Self.

The Holy Spirit through Paul captures this cause and effect in yet another loving warning:

> It is for freedom that Christ has set us free. Stand firm, then, and do not let yourselves be burdened again by a yoke of slavery. (Gal. 5:1)

Jesus freed me from the power of Self, and thus the power of pride. Yet I find I prefer to keep the presence of Self close by. But this proximity of pride keeps me posing and posturing, and I have little peace, and I have little joy.

If I remember to acknowledge Jesus in all my ways—to see Him in all my details—, I find myself being joyful always, naturally praying continually (on and off all day) and then I can more naturally give thanks—to Jesus, not to Sam—in all circumstances. (1Thes. 5:16-18)

Now this is the life to the full Jesus came for you to have.

You can have it. But you must choose this day to remember what C.S. Lewis said:

> He is trying to make you humble in order to make this moment possible: trying to take off a lot of silly, ugly, fancy-dress in which we have all got ourselves up and are strutting about like the little idiots we are.

74

The Rulebook vs.
The Playbook

In sports, there is the rulebook, and there is the play-
book. The rule book is the list of all the things one cannot do. The
rulebook does not list all the things one can do because that is practically limitless. No, the function of the rulebook is to state plainly
what actions are violations and will, therefore, bring penalties and
punishment.

The rulebook doesn't sound like much fun, does it? The rulebook is not on anyone's list of positive things to learn, but we all
know we cannot play a sport without it—nor can we live life without it.

The playbook, on the other hand, contains all the plays the
coach wants his or her players to learn. This is the fun part for the
players. The playbook is what we can do, what we get to do—not
what we cannot do. We all like the playbook. We don't typically
chafe against the playbook, certainly not like we do against the rulebook.

Let's apply this example to your Bible.

First, answer the following questions about the rulebook versus
the playbook:

- Which is a burden, and which a blessing?
- Which is about failure, and which is about freedom?

- Which is more about living Jesus' "life to the full?"

- Which is the Old Testament, and which is the New Testament?

I think we can agree on most, if not all, answers to the above.

The rulebook is always seen in a more negative light and the playbook a more positive. I assume you placed the Old Testament in the rulebook category and the New Testament in the playbook?

But because I have spent these last few Putting Greens seeking to shift your perspective on the scriptures, I am going to challenge your thinking with this next question.

Is the Old Testament book of Leviticus a rulebook or a playbook?

If you have ever tried to read the Bible beginning to end, you have likely run aground in the middle of Leviticus. Many have shipwrecked on the overwhelming list of, "Do *not* do this and this and this and this and this and..."

But!

But right in the middle of this Old Testament rulebook we see two astounding examples of the playbook of life. First, for this week:

> When you reap the harvest of your land, do not reap to the very edges of your field or gather the gleanings of your harvest. Do not go over your vineyard a second time or pick up the grapes that have fallen. Leave them for the poor and the foreigner. I am the Lord your God. (Lev. 19:9-10)

The "Old Testament God of Rules" is laying down a positive playbook play: "When you are gathering your harvest, leave some for the poor, the widows, and the outcasts of your society. Do not pick up every last grape, olive, wheat, fruit or vegetable. No, I want you to leave for others a portion of your hard-earned profit, the harvest you plan to live on; yes, the harvest for which you have worked and worried and waited all season."

Do you see the positive generosity play here from the Author of the Playbook of Life?

This "play" has enhanced my tipping at restaurants and elsewhere. Now when I am calculating a tip, I think to myself, "Will an extra $5.00 or $10.00 really make a difference to me?"

Don't be ridiculous. Of course not. But imagine the difference it makes in the waiter's life. This has become my way of following the rulebook-Leviticus-playbook on generosity.

Imagine that: a positive, fun play right in the middle of the dreaded Old Testament rulebook of Leviticus. And there is more.

75

Life to the Full

In him was life and that life was the light of the world.

—John 1:4

How would you tell the story of your best friend to those who have never met him or her? Would you add more facts and more information? Or would you want to paint a picture of the *Life* that was in him or her? John masterfully paints so much more than a picture; he paints for us a living portrait of Jesus.

John wants you to see how the Jesus who so radically changed the world changed his own life. Because he knows Jesus can change your life, as well. I know this because he changed mine. Slowly at first, then picking up steam as he moved deeper and deeper within me, filling the voids and holes inside me that had plagued me for all those years.

Before Jesus turned the Light on in me I did not know I was so 'holey,' but I knew for sure I was not holy. I was empty inside, but I was so blind I could not see it. I just knew deep down there had to be more. So I tried to fill up on the cotton candy of this world. It tasted good at the time, but I was soon as hungry as before.

I knew there had to be more, so I tried the world's fullness, and came up empty.

I'm guessing you have too.

I do not have to know you to know you are the same. You are human, therefore you were born with a God-shaped hole inside.[1] Okay, you may have performed at such a high level at work or in the community, or raising your family, that no one else can see it. You may have learned how to masterfully mask your holes. You may even have dulled your senses to the point you have fooled yourself into thinking there are no holes. Almost … fooled yourself.

But you know better. You see, if you do not yet have Jesus filling you, in the way only he can, the holes are still there. So when John tells you, "In my friend Jesus was Life," he means the fullest life possible – he means the Life that fills all your holes.

Think about this: God, John the Baptist, and our John the disciple all stated that Jesus' mission was to destroy the work of the devil, and to deal with our sinful condition:

God told Joseph to name his baby boy Jesus, "because he will save his people from their sins." (Matthew 1:21)

John the Baptist said, "Look, the Lamb of God, who takes away the sin of the world! (John 1:29)

John the disciple said, "The reason the Son of God appeared was to destroy the devil's work." (1 John 3:8)

But Jesus himself had a different take on his mission. He said, in essence, and please do not miss this, "The reason I have come, what compels me, my driving purpose, is for you to experience the same Life that I have – that is Life with a capital L."

Jesus stated this plainly: "I have come so that you may have life, and I am talking about life to the full!" (John 10:10 slight paraphrase)

Before I met this Jesus, so full of Life, all I had was the 'little l' life. I didn't know Jesus had such a Life to give. As a matter of fact I was pretty sure whatever life he had to give would be boring and irrelevant to my idea of Life to the Full.

Jesus means it when he tells you, you, my friend, reading this right now, "I have come so that you (fill in your name and say it out loud _____) may start today experiencing my Life to the Full – so full even to the point of overflowing."

Fill up on Jesus, and you will soon overflow with his fullness.

76

10:30 on Tuesdays

I hear this often from men: "I feel so close to Jesus early in the morning when I am reading and praying during my devotional time. But by 10:30 I'm engrossed in work, and I might not think about God or Jesus until that night – if then. How do I bring my early morning quiet time into my busy day?"

Is this not the challenge for all of us? I am in the ministry business and yet I can find myself having been focused on work all morning, and had no conversation with Jesus during that time. Oh sure, I am working on Jesus stuff, but if I am not careful I can slip into "If I don't, it won't" mode in a flash.

But if there is to be any real transformation in my life, I simply must figure out a way to bring Jesus into the details of my hour to hour, day to day, talking and walking around life.

My favorite author puts it like this:

> God wants us to be in a "conversational walk through life," talking with Him about what we are doing together. Then we begin to understand that God's whole purpose is to bring us to the point where He can walk with us quietly, calmly and constantly, leaving us space to grow to be His (often fumbling) collaborators – to have some distance from Him and yet to be united with Him because we are being conformed to the image of His son, bearing the family resemblance. (Dallas Willard, *Hearing God*)

If you would begin this "conversational walk" today, pausing throughout the day to chat with Jesus about what is going on in your life, wouldn't this transform your day? And then your life. And then who you are?

I might even go so far as to say beginning this conversational walk is more important than understanding doctrine and theology. (I'll likely get some emails for that statement.) But I am undaunted in this conviction.

Of course you want to read your Bibles daily. Of course you want to learn and understand the theology and the doctrines that emanate from the scriptures. And yet the value of this conversational walk – at the 10:30's on Tuesdays and the 3:30's on Wednesdays – is absolutely immeasurable.

I heard a story years ago about three holy men who lived on an island, separated from civilization, and therefore "civilized" church doctrine. They were renowned for their powerful prayers and the resulting miracles that accompanied them. But they were simple men, not schooled in the theology and the doctrine of the church.

The Bishop of that region heard about these men and their powerful prayer life, so he decided to visit them. Upon arriving, he asked them to show him how they prayed. The three men began their simple, elemental prayers, but the Bishop soon interrupted them.

He said, "Men, you sound as though you are just having a conversation with God. This won't do. Let me teach you and train you so that your prayers will be more organized and sophisticated." He spent much time with them doing just that. After he was satisfied he got back on his boat and proceeded to sail away.

Shortly he noticed what looked like a fireball coming towards the boat from the direction of the island. Suddenly he realized it was the three holy men running to him on the water.

They exclaimed with great angst, "Your Holiness, we have already forgotten your last outline on prayer! Please teach us again!"

The bishop regarded the men standing on the water, glowing with holiness, and lowered his head and said to them, "Please go home and forget everything I said. Just keep your conversation with Jesus going as before."

So here is another "January challenge:"

May you begin your own personal conversational walk throughout your day – today, yes, today – talking with Jesus about what you are doing together.

It will change your life.

77

Invite—Involve

"If you want things to be different you have to do things differently."

Do you want things to be different? Do you want to keep growing – in all areas of your life – or are you satisfied just coasting? I am frequently looking for ways to bump my trajectory, especially in my walk with Jesus. I use the word "walk" intentionally, because walking is the measure of a life of faith.

The Holy Spirit prompted the prophet Isaiah to write:

> Even youths grow tired and weary, and young men stumble and fall; but those who hope in the Lord will renew their strength. They will soar on wings like eagles; they will run and not grow weary, they will walk and not be faint. (Isa. 40:30-31)

"… they will walk and not be faint."

When I am soaring with emotion on a spiritual high my focus and my devotion to Jesus can be easy. And, I like running because it feeds my inner achievement drive. But to walk, calmly, quietly and constantly with Jesus? This is not so easy, is it? I like movement, I like motion, I like measurable mountains!

But this is not the way of the disciple of Jesus. This is:

> When Christ's abiding presence becomes our guide, then guidance becomes an almost unconscious

response to the gentle moving of His Holy Spirit within us. (Bob Mumford, *Take Another Look at Guidance*)

"The gentle moving of His Holy Spirit within us." But how to live this?

May I suggest you adopt this practice: **Outset – Reset?**

At the outset of each day invite Jesus into your day. Invite him into the details of your day. In the morning I look over my Daytimer and the list of things to do, and I invite Jesus into each meeting, each errand, each task.

Jesus makes a rather remarkable promise about this **Outset: Invite**:

> Here I am! I stand at the door and knock. If anyone hears my voice and opens the door, I will come in and eat with that person, and they with me. (Rev. 3:20)

Are we to take Jesus literally? Is it that simple? I just open the door of my heart and in he comes?

Yes.

But you must mean it and you must want it. Perhaps your prayer may just be, "Jesus help me to want to want to invite you in." He knows your heart. He is not expecting you to be perfect – even in your "wanting." You open the door of your heart; he will take care of the coming in part.

This is a wonderful start to your day. If you start this practice – and it will take practice – it will change your day. And it will change … transform … you.

78

Reset: Involve

If I want to go deeper in my relationship with my best friend and Savior, I must find a way to involve him in my day to day life – in the details. I have a friend who, when she went off to college, missed her boyfriend so much she wrote him a note every day. She would just write down her thoughts on and off throughout the day, and then send them all together as one letter about once a week.

I remember vividly her thoughts on this practice: "It just makes me feel closer to him. I feel like he is with me throughout each day."

Isn't this a perfect example of what we want with Jesus? At least I hope you want this. Jesus does for you. But how to do this?

Last week we began a look at adopting this practice: **Outset – Reset.**

At the outset of each day invite Jesus into your day. Invite him into the details of your day. In the morning take a look at your list of things to do and invite Jesus, and the Holy Spirit, into each meeting, each errand, each task.

This is a wonderful start to your day. And yet, what about the rest of the day? The "10:30's on Tuesdays?" How to continue this invitation into and throughout the day?

I try to make a practice of **Reset: Involve** at various times throughout the day. I pause to reset my focus by purposely involving the Holy Spirit in my schedule. I have to purposely do this because I am no different than you. I get distracted. I get tunnel-vision and Self starts to take over.

When this happens I can feel my neck and shoulders tightening up. I can sense my focus becoming more and more myopic. I don't like this, and I don't want this. I don't want Sam to take over – even with the best of intentions.

So I pause, I take a deep breath, and I reset my focus by again inviting Jesus and the Holy Spirit into whatever it is I am doing. By doing this I am following the teaching of Jesus:

> Therefore everyone who hears these words of mine and puts them into practice is like a wise man who built his house on the rock. (Matt. 7:24)

So I put into practice these encouraging words from Jesus:

> Come to me. Get away with me and you will recover your life. Walk with me and work with me – watch how I do it. Learn the unforced rhythms of grace. Keep company with me and you will learn to live freely and lightly. (Matt. 11:28-30, MSG. See below is the NIV version[1])

"Learn the unforced rhythms of grace."

This is what I seek. This is what I crave. And so do you. I know this without necessarily having to know you.

By the way, my conversation and my invitation each morning begins with Jesus, yes, but I am learning to actually invite and ask for the Holy Spirit's involvement. Jesus is my best friend, but the Holy Spirit is my power source. He leads me, He guides me, and He empowers me, just as Jesus promised he would. We call this Holy Spirit power: Energy – Clarity – Creativity.

I need this each day, and throughout each day. Don't you?

Won't you try this? Be purposeful and intentional about this, **"Outset: Invite and Reset: Involve,"** because ... you will have to be. It will not come naturally. But the reward will be to change your day – and then to transform you.

[1] Come to me, all you who are weary and burdened, and I will give you rest. Take my yoke upon you and learn from me, for I am gentle and humble in heart, and you will find rest for your souls. For my yoke is easy and my burden is light. (Matt. 11:28-30)

79

The Armor of the 4 P's

We have previously talked about starting each day with an invitation to Jesus to be a part of your day, and then at various times throughout the day pausing, to reset your focus, by involving him in what you are currently doing. We call it **Outset: Invite – Reset: Involve.**

This week I want to give you a tool to assist you in this. I call this, "The Armor of the 4 P's."

1. Perspective

Start each day by reminding yourself the Holy Spirit is right there with you. You are in his presence. And he is in yours.

When Jesus starts his famous prayer with, "Our Father in heaven," he actually says, "Our Father in the heavens." The ... *heavens.* Jesus is saying God Almighty's presence starts with and in the air around you. You live in a God-saturated world.

The image we have of Jesus sitting at the right hand of God out there somewhere beyond the stars, in heaven somewhere off in space—as Bette Midler sang, *"From A Distance"* —is absolutely ridiculous. You are surrounded by God. You are hemmed in by Jesus. The Holy Spirit is always with you.

Start your day with this perspective of His always-presence, and then reset your perspective throughout the day to remind you of this ... fact.

2. Purpose

I typically wrestle with one of three purposes each day:

1. My purpose
2. Inviting and involving the Holy Spirit into … my purpose.
3. Wanting to be invited and involved in the Holy Spirit's purpose for me.

The first is all about Sam and Self.

The second is an improvement, but it is still ultimately about my purpose.

The third is a matter of the heart. I still have my list of things to do each day—my Daytimer for next week is already full—but I reset my heart to be open to his interruptions, his pop-ins, his shifts – i.e. his purpose.

Yes, each day I follow my Daytimer, but I am first following Jesus, so I am ready and open to his purposes throughout the day.

3. Priority

Jesus promises, actually he guarantees that if he is my top priority, he will get involved with the details of my day, and in the process help me with all the things I need.

> So do not worry, saying, 'What shall we eat?' or 'What shall we drink?' or 'What shall we wear?' … But seek first his kingdom and his righteousness, and all these things will be given to you as well. (Matthew 6:31 & 33)

"Seeking first" is a matter of the heart. If I start each day with our **Outset: Invite,** and during the day I practice **Reset: Involve,** I will more and more naturally seek first the Kingdom of God, and not the kingdom of Sam.

Regrettably, I believe it is a binary priority choice: The Kingdom of God or Sam's kingdom.

4. Power

Each day I have a choice as to which power source I choose. I can rely on Sam's power, or I can ask for, and lean into, the power of the Holy Spirit. My power or His power—or yours?

We are promised an incredible Holy Spirit power source by Jesus:

> But you will receive power when the Holy Spirit comes
> on you. (Acts 1:8)

And Jesus said we will actually be better off, and do greater works than him, with this Holy Spirit power. That is an astounding promise! (See John 14:12 & 16:7)

To sum up: "If you want things to be different" —and I hope you do— "you have to do things differently."

This begins not just *doing* differently, although it certainly involves this, but *being* different. By starting each day putting on the full armor of the 4 P's: your Perspective, his Purpose, his Priority and his Power source.

80

Water to Wine

*Now to him who is able to do immeasurably more than all
we ask or imagine.*

—Eph. 3:20

Jesus is at a wedding, having fun, when his mother Mary
tells him the wine is out.

Jesus answers a need with eight hundred bottles of choice wine.
Eight Hundred! Is this perhaps a tad over the top? Perhaps. But it is
not unusual for Jesus. After all, when he takes a few fish and a little
bread and feeds five thousand men, plus their families, he still has
twelve baskets overflowing with extra bread.

> They all ate and were satisfied, and the disciples picked
> up twelve basketfuls of broken pieces that were left
> over. (Luke 9:17)

When he decided to get Peter's attention he almost sunk two
boats with so many fish:

> When he had finished speaking, he said to Simon, "Put
> out into deep water, and let down the nets for a catch."
> … When they had done so, they caught such a large

number of fish that their nets began to break. So they signaled their partners in the other boat to come and help them, and they came and filled both boats so full that they began to sink. (Luke 5:4,6-7)

How Jesus Does Things

Let's think for a moment about the choices Jesus had in this whole wedding affair.

1. He could have not gone at all. He is after all the long awaited Messiah. He has much to do to kick off his ministry. But Jesus is a relational God.

2. He could have said no to Mary.

Please do not miss this: Jesus never says no, as in "No, I won't respond at all to your need."

He may say, "No, I won't answer your specific request—because it would not be the best path for you," but he always responds, and always in the best way possible.

Now, as to how he could have responded with respect to the Quantity & Quality of wine:

3. He could have produced just barely enough wine, and ordinary wine at that. This would have saved the young bride and groom. And yet they would still worry about running out, again.

4. He could have produced more than enough wine, and perhaps this time a better quality, yet still just an above average wine.

5. But remember, Jesus is no bread and water God. He responds with an Ephesians 3:20, "immeasurably more than all we ask or imagine," wine.

And he will with you, too. To be sure my Ephesians 3:20 answer will look different from yours, but it will be just right for me, and just right for you. Yes, his way and his timing may try our patience. But Jesus always responds with immeasurably more than all we ask, or even imagine to ask, and always in just the perfect, customized response to your need and to mine.

That is how Jesus does things.

But my question to you is this:

When you approach Jesus with your prayers, and your needs, which of the above 1. – 5. responses do you expect? Do you think he won't even show up, or will say no, or will at best respond with just barely enough, and ordinary at that?

My friend, may you learn that Jesus always responds with immeasurably more than all we ask, or even imagine to ask, and may the eyes of your heart be enlightened so you may see his response for the Ephesians 3:20 gift it always is.

81

The Crutch

Recently I overhead someone say, "So many of these 'Born-Again' types just need Christianity as a crutch." I have heard this many times, and said it myself more than once, back before I realized how badly I needed a crutch.

So let's explore this idea of a crutch today. Take for example someone who is blind and lame. They have been struggling for years trying to get around: hobbling, tripping, falling down, bruising and scraping their face and skin repeatedly. They bump into obstacles constantly, and many times have taken the wrong way home.

They cannot possibly see the best way, and if even they could, they cannot follow this best way with any consistency. Problems and pain are a constant result of their blind, lame condition. Problems and pain for themselves, as well as for those around them.

Now, let me pause and say this: This describes me perfectly, before I met Jesus. And quite frankly even for years after—when I still could not see with any true clarity, and I was still stumbling around with residual lameness.

Does this describe you?

Yes, that was me! I may have appeared to have it all together, and to be smart and athletic and all that. But in reality I was a blind, lame sinner. I was so blind and so lame I didn't even know it. So I looked down on those who had found Jesus, and condescendingly thought of them as weak for needing a crutch.

Now imagine someone comes along and offers this blind, lame person a crutch. We all know this crutch will stabilize their balance and enable them to move through life with a newfound purpose, and help them to avoid so many problems and pains.

What must a person be like to turn down this offer of this crutch? I can think of two words: stupid and prideful. Of course, pride-filled people are inherently stupid. As was I.

What perhaps might such a person say in response to the offer of a crutch?

"Oh, I don't need a crutch! Crutches are for those pathetic losers. I am fine and dandy just like I am. Actually, better than just fine and dandy, just like I am. I don't need a crutch."

Stupid.

Or, perhaps, "Are you kidding? Me, accept a crutch? Why I'd sooner limp around my whole life than be seen as someone who needed that kind of help."

Prideful.

Now please hear this: Following Jesus is so much more than a crutch; it is the only choice to make in life. He is it—there is nothing else. The crutch is there at the start, yes, but it then morphs into a rock-solid foundation upon which we now can live our lives grounded on the rock of Jesus, and not the shifting sands of Self, stupidity and pride.

The previously much needed crutch dissipates, as does the lameness and the blindness, and we find ourselves running and jumping, and seeing life in a whole new light. Like a newborn foal finding its legs, standing up for the first time, then starting to run around, kicking up its hind legs.

This new life is infused with light, energy, joy, balance and stability.

Now, you might need a crutch. If you don't have Jesus, you absolutely do. Are you too stupid or too prideful to accept it?

> Therefore everyone who hears these words of mine and puts them into practice is like a wise man who built his house on the rock. The rain came down, the streams rose, and the winds blew and beat against that house;

yet it did not fall, because it had its foundation on the rock. But everyone who hears these words of mine and does not put them into practice is like a foolish man who built his house on sand. The rain came down, the streams rose, and the winds blew and beat against that house, and it fell with a great crash. (Matt. 7:24-27)

82

Abandon the Outcome to Jesus

I am constantly proclaiming that I am the luckiest man on the planet. I hope you want to argue with me, and claim that I am not, because you are. But if you do not think you are, I am confident that after we sat together for ten minutes, I could show you that you indeed are.

Why do I feel like the luckiest man on the planet?

> I thank Christ Jesus our Lord, who has given me strength, that he considered me trustworthy, appointing me to his service. Even though I was once a blasphemer and a persecutor and a violent man, I was shown mercy because I acted in ignorance and unbelief. The grace of our Lord was poured out on me abundantly, along with the faith and love that are in Christ Jesus. (1 Tim. 1:12-14)

My hope is that you, too, can say this with conviction and with sincerity.

Without having his grace poured out on me abundantly, along with the faith and love that are in Christ Jesus, I would be, I could only be, perhaps mildly happy, and only sporadically lucky.

But there is another step in becoming so lucky: Learning to abandon the outcome to Jesus. My friend, you must learn to do this.

You must! It is the key to the life that is truly life. When you learn to take your hands off the outcome, to loosen your grip, to stop trying to control the outcome, God's grace and peace will indeed be poured out on you abundantly.

Grace and peace. You will sense it, you will see it, and trust me, those around you will see it, too. They will praise Jesus for such an astounding miracle! When you relax your grip, Jesus' peace will begin to flow in you and through you, and soon enough it will flow out of you, onto and into those around you.

This is in part what Jesus meant when he said, "Streams of living water will flow from within you." (John 7:38)

But you must learn to abandon the outcome to Jesus. I could say, "Learn to 'let go of' the outcome," but *abandon* carries a sense of total release. As in, "I turned my back on the outcome!"

Next week we will discuss the difference between abandoning the outcome and abandoning the process. We do not abandon the process–we do our part. We do our very best part.

But hear this, you do not control the outcome. This C-19 mess should have convinced you of this...fact. You never have controlled the outcome, and you never will. If you think you do, you are deluded. And no doubt the people around you are suffering. Because when you are sure you can control the outcome, you white-knuckle everything and everyone, maintaining an ever-tightening grip, driving yourself and everyone around you nuts.

I had a man tell me once, "Sam, this new career is very stressful. In my previous job I could control the outcome. But now I have no control at all over the outcome."

I looked at him and smiled and said, "John, you never controlled the outcome in your last job. You just thought you did, because perhaps most things went your way."

A few months later he pulled me aside and said, "What an idiot I must have seemed to you when I made that last statement. I see now I do not, and I cannot, control anything: not my wife, my work, my health, not even my children."

Another friend, a nice person, but a true control freak, had several things turn upside down in his life. I bumped into him recently and he said, "Sam, I am learning I do not have the control I thought

I had. As you know, I was driving a pretty big bus (his business, investments, and his family), but I white-knuckled that bus right into a ditch. Now I am learning to loosen my grip on the steering wheel."

Oswald Chambers captures this perfectly:

> If you totally abandon yourself to God, He immediately says to you, "I will give your life to you as a prize." The reason people are tired of life is that God has not given them anything—they have not been given their life as a prize.
>
> The way to get out of that condition is to abandon yourself to God. And once you do get to the point of total surrender to Him, you will be the most surprised and delighted person on earth. (*My Utmost For His Highest*, April 28)

83

Abandon the Outcome . . . Not the Process

I get really excited talking about abandoning the out-
come to Jesus. This is because I have learned over the years that failing to do this becomes the source of most of my stress and anxiety.
These thoughts then take over:

"What will I do if this doesn't work out...my way?"
"How will I...What if ...Who will...?"

And the famous rallying cry of control nuts:

"If I don't, it won't!" "If it is to be, it is up to me!"

But there is another way. A quieter, calmer, more relaxed way.
It is the way of the Savior.

> Come to me, all you who are weary and burdened, and
> I will give you rest. Take my yoke upon you and learn
> from me, for I am gentle and humble in heart, and you
> will find rest for your souls. For my yoke is easy and
> my burden is light. (Matt. 11:28-30)

Simply put, let Jesus help. Let him be a part of the process. Involve him. Invite him in, not just to try to get the outcome you desire, but invite him into the process–and you will find rest for your
souls.

You see, even though we abandon the outcome to Jesus, we do
not abandon the process. We have a role to play in the process. A

big role! We do our part, and this can include being competitive, proactive, purposeful, even shrewd and creative. We use our business acumen, our experience, our judgement, to advance the process.

God does not advocate we sit in a closet, pray and expect him to take care of our lives. Or our children or our businesses. Quite the opposite. Consider these passages:

> But by the grace of God I am what I am, and his grace to me was not without effect. No, I worked harder than all of them—yet not I, but the grace of God that was with me. (1 Cor. 1:10)

> His divine power has given us everything we need for a Godly life through our knowledge of him who called us by his own glory and goodness...For this very reason, make every effort to add to your faith.... (2 Peter 1:3 & 5)

Paul and Peter first state that the source of their power comes from God. But they are then quick to point out that we are to "work harder than all of them," and we are to "make every effort...." And yet we find a surprising rest for our souls in the midst of our efforts and hard work, because we have involved Jesus in the process.

We combine our effort with the presence and power of Jesus through the Holy Spirit, and together—*together*—we proceed through the process. All the while knowing with absolute certainty we cannot do it on our own. As a matter of fact, a great milestone in my life with Jesus was when I realized, "I do not even want to do it on my own."

Please do not miss that. When you can grow to this point, where you do not even want to do it on your own, you are kicking it into high gear. Remember, there is a quieter, calmer, more relaxed way. It is the way of the Savior. Oswald Chambers captures this other way perfectly:

A Christian is someone who trusts in the knowledge and the wisdom of God, not in his own abilities. If we have a purpose of our own, it destroys the simplicity and the calm, relaxed pace which should be characteristic of the children of God. (*My Utmost For His Highest*, August 5)

Do you have a calm, relaxed pace? Both inside and out?

If we have a purpose, an outcome of our own, then we are not trusting that our Heavenly Father's outcome will be better, richer than ours. And instead of abandoning the outcome, we have abandoned the calm, relaxed pace that should, and could be characteristic of a trusting child of God.

84

Peace and Pace in the Process

We have been talking about abandoning the outcome to Jesus. I could spend a year on this because it is that important. Until you learn to do so, you simply will not live with the peace Jesus promised His followers.

To be blunt, if you are not abandoning the outcome, you are not following Jesus. You are following your own ability and your own purpose and your own required outcome. I lived that way for years–and for years I coped with the accompanying stress by medicating myself with various "stress-reducers."

But no more. And the freedom that comes with this release, well, it is a peace that passes all understanding.

Peace in the Pace

Last week we were very clear: We abandon the outcome, but not the process. Today, I want to touch on the peace we can find within the pace of the process. As we move forward in our pursuit of our goals and objectives, for our business, family or personal, we allow the peace of Jesus to be a guardrail–or even a stop sign–during the process.

When we feel ourselves stressing during the process, and wanting to press the pace even faster, we slow down, have a conversation with Jesus, and ask for His guidance through the Holy Spirit.

As an example, I will share with you an 'F' on my part with respect to abandoning, and an 'A+' on my daughter Britton's part.

A few years ago, Britton was relocating to Jacksonville for work. Dina and I met her there for the purpose of finding a place to live. We had one weekend to accomplish this. A quick pace indeed.

The first three places were within Britton's budget, but Dad did not want her living in any of them. Even though I was assured they were safe, they looked like Beirut ghetto neighborhoods to me.

The fourth place was perfect! Much bigger, with decks and porches and bigger rooms. The rent was a tad more than Britton had budgeted, but who cares–I was 100% in favor. But Britton was not, and kept saying, "Dad, I just don't have a peace about this. I am going to continue to ask the Holy Spirit for guidance and clarity until I do."

My response? "I have already checked with the Holy Spirit and He tells me this is the perfect place." (Argh)

That night over dinner Britton continued to express her hesitation, and the check in her spirit, and I continued to express my approval of the place, and to tell her to ignore this check in her spirit, and listen to her wise father. I reminded Britton, as I played the Holy Spirit, we needed to make a choice by the next day.

But she demurred.

The next morning, she attended a church that some friends had recommended. After the service she was introduced to the young pastor and his family. It "just so happened," by "pure coincidence," they had a pool house they were looking to rent.

Here are the results of Britton's abandoning the outcome, but seeking peace during the fast weekend pace of the process:

1. The rent was much less than her budgeted amount.

2. The pool house was tucked safely behind the young pastor's home in a safe neighborhood. And she had access to their pool.

3. The young pastor's family became family to Britton, and Boyd, the young pastor, was part of Britton's wedding.

4. She had an instant community and instant church home.

5. And most important, Dad was able to rest assured for the next three years his precious daughter was safe and sound, and surrounded by wonderful families and friends.

Well, actually the most important part was Jesus was glorified, because of Britton's trust in His involvement in the details of her life.

Please do not miss that. Because she trusted that Jesus was deeply involved in the details of her life, even to the point of assisting in this house search, she was able to abandon the outcome to Him, and to seek, and therefore find, His peace through the pace of the process.

That is the A+ life that is truly life.

85

Pause to Transition

Years ago, I read an interview with Jack Nicklaus, in which he was asked about the key to his enormous success. His response knocked me out of my seat. I will paraphrase it here:

> I realized early on that tournaments are won and lost on the putting green. So I trained myself to pause before stepping onto the green, gather myself, and get hyper-focused.

We spend all day on the fairway of life. The fairway is important, but the most important time is when we arrive home to our family. We are stepping up onto the putting green, where the tournament of life is won or lost.

So I began to train myself to pull the car over before getting home, gather myself, and get hyper-focused for my family. No more of this, "I need some me time." No more of this, "I am exhausted from a hard day, so I am irritable and impatient."

No!

That is unacceptable. And you are losing the game of life, whether you know it or not. But I can guarantee you, your spouse and children know it.

You need a transition from your fairway-day to putting green time with your family.

In his excellent book, *Get Your Life Back*, John Eldredge talks about pausing throughout the day, and transitioning from one task to the next. If you are like me, you motor from one to the next to the next, all the while answering voicemails, texts, emails, and checking your newsfeeds.

But I am learning to transition. Here are two recent examples, one a win and one a whiff, of how I am trying to pause and transition.

A Win

Recently I visited my dear friend Hank, who has ALS. We had a marvelous time together. His wit is always delightful, and his self-effacing approach to his condition always surprises me.

Afterward, I got in my car, with sports talk radio already on, and proceeded to head to my next appointment. But a voice reminded me, "Stop, Sam, you knucklehead, and absorb what just happened. Slow down, and reflect for a moment."

And I did. I paused to transition before the next meeting and phone calls and emails and texts. I reflected on this man who is in the grips of ALS, and yet smiled our entire conversation. He had me laughing in stitches several times. What grace. What strength. What perseverance under fire.

As I paused for this transition, my perspective started to shift, and the importance of my problems diminished. I slowed down. My gratitude for the gift of my friendship with Hank swelled and my hurried heart slowed down and softened. How could I just jet off to the next to-do list item, without a transition from that most sacred time?

A Whiff

Last night my daughter, Britton, taught a lesson on Grace to one hundred plus ladies via Zoom. It was an excellent presentation, and far beyond anything I could have done at her age. While she was teaching, I marveled at the sight of my little girl, so deep in her relationship with Jesus, and so deep in her understanding of grace.

But it was Monday night, and I had a stack of bills to pay. So immediately afterward I jumped on that stack of bills and starting writing checks. It needed to get done!

No transition. No reflection on the joy of watching one's little girl, as a grown-up woman leading other women. I missed it. I whiffed on the transition. But I am learning, and at least the Holy Spirit got my attention this morning.

Pauses help me to slow down for a few moments, which provide a much-needed transition, and in doing so, to allow my heart and my soul to fill up with the depth of the   experience. Not just blow right through it.

May you, my friend, find a way to learn to pause throughout your day, refill your soul's tank, and transition from one task to the next, not frenetically, but thoughtfully and gracefully.

86

Release and Restore

Two weekends ago we attended a YWAM (Youth with A Mission) conference in Colorado Springs. The featured speaker for Thursday and Friday nights was John Eldredge – a well known and loved Christian writer. His most recognized book is Wild at Heart.

What I did not know is John is a therapist by profession. As he stepped up to begin his talk that Thursday night, I was expecting just that – a talk, a presentation, perhaps an outline and teaching session. I could not have been more wrong.

He began by saying, "I have been asking the Lord what message to bring to you all, and the word I keep getting is 'mercy.' Mercy in the sense that you all need to give yourself mercy in these trying times, and learn to … release and restore … your very souls."

Well, with his emphasis on "release and restore," he had my immediate attention. I have been talking to the 721 men about release and restore with respect to forgiving others – and you can listen to our thirty-minute videos on these at our YouTube channel at 721ministries.org   at   https://www.youtube.com/channel/UCJj3hsuJyYVMsmvRdfG6sIg.

But I had not thought about the importance of releasing and restoring ourselves.

And then he said this:

"Trauma has many elements, but three common aspects to trauma are these:

1. "Your norm, your normal life, is ripped out from under you.

2. "After that everything keeps shifting and changing.

3. "You are exposed to violence."

Now my friends, does this sound familiar? Just ponder our last eight months. Our normal life has been turned upside down; the rules and guidelines keep shifting, making it impossible to return to any sort of norm; we are watching violence on TV practically every day. Some of us have experienced it first-hand.

You are traumatized, whether you recognize it or not. Of course, the men will push back on this and pretend to be macho and manly about it, but you ladies can receive this more readily. So men, stop being knuckleheads and open up to the idea that you cannot just put your head down and bull your way through this chaos.

When John Eldredge finished that first night, he asked for comments or questions, and I raised my hand and said, "I thought you would give us a fine talk, perhaps with a power point outline and all that, but I did not expect a therapy session. And I did not know how much I needed one!"

There was nervous laughter around the room and several "Amens."

I am out of town this week, so I plan to share his comments more fully with you next week, but today I strongly recommend you do three things.

The first is to listen to our thirty minute video talk on his "therapy session" at our YouTube channel at: https://www.youtube.com/watch?v=V41gp2ZmZm8

The second is to download John's app: "One Minute Pause." It is free and has been a trajectory bump for me. The app is much more than just a reminder to pause during the day; it provides a refreshing and refilling transition during your otherwise busy day.

Do not just blow this off – like I probably would. This "pause" app has become an essential part of my day. https://apps.apple.com/us/app/one-minute-pause/id1471913620

The third is to read his book, *Get Your Life Back*.

More on this next week, but please do not be in the 80% that will not do any of these three things, because I guarantee you your time will be well invested if you at least do the first two.

87

Reject to Protect

*Come to me, all you who are weary and burdened, and I will
give you rest. Take my yoke upon you and learn from me,
for I am gentle and humble in heart, and **you will find rest
for your souls**."*

—Matt. 11:28-29, bold added

I previously introduced the idea of restoring our souls
in this crazy, soul-scorching world in which we live. There is very
little, if anything, in this culture that will draw you closer to Jesus.
Everything is designed, not necessarily to draw you away from Jesus, but to draw you towards something else – specifically what
they are selling, be it merchandise or ideas. The result is a soul separated from its Source.

We are all in a quest for peace, a search for soul rest. We just
perhaps do not realize it. C.S. Lewis said your soul is a vessel for
God to fill. Well, if He is to fill it, we must be proactive in plugging
the holes this culture is pricking in it.

This was John Eldredge's message to us in Colorado Springs
recently. We must take care of our souls, and our souls are currently
under constant attack. Each time you open your news feed, each
time you check Fox News or CNN, each time you open up Twitter
or Facebook, or turn on your TV, Social Media, movies, or whatever,

you are venturing into "Destination: Distraction and Discouragement."

Now some of you are rolling your eyes, thinking I am exaggerating the issues, or that you – you being the only one! – are not affected by any of this. But consider this: A British archeologist did an extensive study of cultures and communities, and how they relate to the size and development of our brains. His scientific conclusion is that our brains – and I would add our souls – are only designed to handle a community of 150 people.

Let that sit for a moment.

Think about it, until very recently this would have been the norm. It is just recently that we have been exposed to every woe, every evil, every misfortune that is happening around the globe. The first worldwide TV broadcast was the moon landing in 1969. And even after that it was years before we were watching in our living rooms disasters taking place in Bangladesh.

And now you are watching it in the palm of your hand. And it is crushing your soul, whether you know it, or whether you acknowledge it. Your soul was not designed to handle a worldwide community.

As we were flying out to Colorado, I hit my news feed, which I am … *was* … wont to do, and saw four hundred whales beached on a coastline somewhere, in a freak act of nature. So, four hundred dead and rotting whales accompanied me out to CO, their vivid picture lodged in my brain. They were joined by news of a horrible killing, a loving husband dying while trying to save his child, and a young girl kidnapped and raped.

My soul withered in the face of this onslaught. All right there in the palm of my hand. But I did not know it. Not until John Eldredge pointed this out to me, was I even aware of what I was doing to myself. *Doing to myself, mind you.* I was numb to it all.

Did you know the average person looks at their cell phone eighty times a day? Not you, of course, but the average person. I am sure it is … *was* … me.

No more!

I am putting into practice measures to break the hold my cell phone has on me. Here are the guardrails I am erecting to protect me from careening off into the cataract of the cacophony of this culture.

1. I do not even turn my phone over until I have finished my time with Jesus in the morning. I keep it face down.

2. I only look at it every thirty minutes – on the hour and half hour.

3. At 8:00 pm it goes down again.

Emails and texts will have to wait until the hour and the half hour during the day. By the way, I asked a couple of my attorney friends, men who live and die on their phones, if they could survive on my new thirty-minute email and text check. Their first response was incredulous. I thought their heads would explode. But in just a moment they each said, "Yes, I absolutely could."

You can too, you know.

If you will reject the cataract of the culture, *you will find rest for your souls*.

88

Release to Protect

This is what the Lord says:
"Stand at the crossroads and look;
*   ask for the ancient paths,*
ask where the good way is, and walk in it,
*   and you will find rest for your souls."*

—Jer. 6:16

We are all seeking rest for our souls. Most of us, and I
would say all of us, do not even know we are. We do not even know
how wearied our souls are. We numb our souls with caffeine, a little
wine at 5:00, TV, social media, and our ever-present smart phones.
And just FYI, your soul is simply not designed to move at the speed
of your smart phone.[1]

After our weekend with John Eldredge in Colorado Springs, I
feel as though I have been born again, again. I am putting into practice practices that are protecting my soul. Last week we talked about
the practice of rejecting the culture's continuous distractions and di-
versions. We must learn to stiff-arm the assailing assault of the silly.

But that is preventative maintenance. We must first do some
initial emptying out of the culture's clutter that we have already,
although unwittingly, allowed to stick in our souls.

The goal is to seek more of Jesus in more of us.[2]

But how?

The Holy Spirit, through Peter, advises us to, "Cast all your anxiety on him because he cares for you" (1 Pet. 5:7). Peter, being a fisherman, uses the Greek word for 'cast,' meaning to throw a net away from a boat. What a splendid picture for us. Cast all those worries, the cares of this world, the junk you have allowed into your soul, the resentments and disappointments, out of your soul. Throw them out and away, as if you are throwing a net away from your boat.

We must release what has stuck inside us over the years. We must empty out so we can fill up with the love, joy, and peace of Jesus. We want to seek more of Jesus in more of us. C.S. Lewis said your soul is a vessel for God to fill. Well, if He is to fill it, we must be proactive in emptying out what we are already full of.

St. Augustine agrees with me (and my bad grammar):

> We must empty ourselves of all that fills us so that we
> may be filled with what we are empty of.

But I want you to notice what Peter is telling us to do with what we are casting away. *Cast all your anxiety ... on him ...* onto Jesus. This is different from just casting away, from just emptying out, as if into thin air. If we try to just cast our anxieties out and away, they are likely to boomerang right back.

But if we cast them onto Jesus, onto his shoulders, and if we trust that we can do this because "he cares for you," then our stuff will better stick with him, and not boomerang back to us.

When I cast all my cares onto Jesus, I am saying to him, "You must take this, Jesus. I cannot control this, and I cannot fix this. And I know my soul cannot carry this load. But I know you can, and I know you will."

This will not happen the first time. You will have to cast away, and cast away, and cast away. Release, release, and release. It will take practice. But as we learn to trust him with our stuff, to trust that he can and is handling them, then it is as if Jesus dumps them into the deepest part of the ocean, and sticks a "No fishing" sign in that spot for us.

And then we are free to seek more of Jesus in more of us.

---

[1] John Eldredge, *Get Your Life Back*
[2] John Eldredge, *Get Your Life Back*

89

Meaningless to Meaning-full

I hope you have read the previous two Putting Greens, as these are all fitting together.

We assume King Solomon wrote Ecclesiastes. He is looking back over his life, and all his accomplishments, and finding them "meaningless." Now that is something we all want to avoid.

I highly recommend you read Ecclesiastes, and remember as you read that this is an older man assessing the value of all the activities that kept him busy all his life, only to realize those activities now hold no value to him—zero value. All eternally insignificant. He states unequivocally,

> Yet when I surveyed all that my hands had done
> and what I had toiled to achieve,
> everything was meaningless, a chasing after the wind;
> nothing was gained under the sun.

Ugh.

Meaningless, a chasing after the wind, under the sun: these are repeated throughout. On my first reading of Ecclesiastes many years ago, I was put off by all the negativity. On my second reading I started to see the warnings. On the many subsequent readings I now see it as a "warning-encouragement."

A warning not to miss what is most important; an encouragement to pursue what is.

As I read Solomon's lament, I can hear Jesus' warning-encouragement:

What good will it be for someone to gain the whole world, yet forfeit their soul? Or what can anyone give in exchange for their soul? (Matt. 16:26)

So how do we avoid this chasing after meaningless things … under the sun? "Under the sun" in Solomon's Jewish world means, "The world in which we live." Above the sun is heaven, the Kingdom of God, where God lives. Jesus' primary mission is to bring these two worlds together:

… your kingdom come your will be done, on earth as it is in heaven. (Matt. 6:10)

Jesus proclaimed repeatedly,

Repent, for the kingdom of heaven has come near … has arrived. (Matt. 4:17)

I can just hear Jesus saying, "Open your eyes, turn from your meaningless ways under the sun. I am here to weave Heaven into your world so there is no longer any separation, and your life becomes a life of eternal significance."

So how can we join Jesus in his quest, so his quest becomes ours? Clearly there are many things we must do each week that hardly seem to rate eternal significance. What to do?

We stop, or at least cut back on the meaningless activities, and we bring meaning to the otherwise meaningless. Stop and ponder that for a moment.

I do not have to know you to know there are activities in your life that could be eliminated. For some they are "untoward" activities, and for some they may be good, but are far, far from the best.

Stop those, now. You can, you know. You have my permission.

The other stuff? Your job, your daily and weekly responsibilities, even your fun hobbies and social activities—we are not advocating you become a no-fun monk: find a way to bring meaning to them. Eternal significance.

Perhaps a kind word. Compassion. Interrupting your all-important to-do schedule. Writing a note. A phone call. Pray *with* someone, *not just for them*. Mention your faith, your friendship with Jesus, in otherwise "news, weather and sports" conversations. (At least mention Jesus from time to time!)

You do not need me to train you in this. Follow your heart—as it is guided by the Holy Spirit. Ask the Holy Spirit to give you energy, clarity and creativity as you ponder this quest to bring meaning to the meaningless. He will.

You can do this. Start today. Then, when the time comes, which may be much sooner than you think, you will hear these most wonderful words,

> Well done, good and faithful servant! You have been faithful with a few things; I will put you in charge of many things. Come and share your master's happiness! (Matt. 25:23)

90

Do Not Take This Lightly

And when I think, that God, His Son not sparing;
Sent Him to die, I scarce can take it in;
That on a Cross, my burdens gladly bearing,
He bled and died to take away my sin.

Then sings my soul, My Saviour God, to Thee,
How great Thou art, How great Thou art.

"I scarce can take it in."

I was reading through the book of Hebrews and was stung, taken aback, by a warning at chapter 10:29:

> How much more severely do you think someone deserves to be punished who has trampled the Son of God underfoot, who has treated as an unholy thing the blood of the covenant that sanctified them, and who has insulted the Spirit of grace?

"To trample underfoot, and to treat as an unholy thing," means to consider something common, nothing special, to give it no value in your life. Or even worse, to consider it worthless.

As we approach Easter and the sacrifice Jesus made for you and for me, I want to challenge you to consider this warning seriously.

(If I were writing to only the men in the 721 meetings, I would say it more bluntly, with a Southern colloquialism: "I hope this slaps you upside the head." 😊)

The Holy Spirit is warning us not to take lightly the sacrifice Jesus offered and the blood he shed on that cross. It is as if God is saying, "After what my son endured for you, the beatings, the bloody, horrific whipping, the horror of the hours while suffocating to death on that cross—if you take a casual, ho-hum approach to him, if you just give him an hour or so a week, and then go about your business as if it is all about you … I will be greatly offended. Greatly."

Again, I can hear God saying, "My son took on himself your sins, he took your blame, he took your shame, naked and humiliated, and you just give him a few minutes a day, or a prayer when you're worried, and then you ignore him, not wanting him to interfere with your busy schedule?"

Are you treating as nothing special Jesus' sacrifice for you? Are you ignoring him for the most part of each day? Not intentionally, of course, but the end result is still the same. Do not fall into the trap of the second or third soils:

> The seed falling on rocky ground refers to someone who hears the word and at once receives it with joy. But since they have no root, they last only a short time.
> The seed falling among the thorns refers to someone who hears the word, but the worries of this life and the deceitfulness of wealth choke the word, making it unfruitful. (Matt. 13:20-21)

Be honest with yourself. The stakes are so high. The rewards are so great. Does the fact that Jesus gave his life for you—gave his life *for you*—change your day to day life? At least even some of the details each day … at least some days?

As Easter approaches, I implore you to embrace Jesus, to think deeply about what he did for you, what he offers you, and to begin to bring him into every detail of your life. Make it personal. Make him personal.

Then let your soul sing out,

> O Lord my God, When I in awesome wonder,
> Consider all the worlds Thy Hands have made;
> I see the stars, I hear the rolling thunder,
> Thy power throughout the universe displayed.
>
> Then sings my soul, My Saviour God, to Thee,
> How great Thou art, How great Thou art.

91

Spirit Over Letter

In his Sermon on the Mount, after his Beatitudes and before he launches into the meat of his talk, Jesus pauses, and so will we. He pauses to introduce his main teaching by saying this:

> Do not think that I have come to abolish the Law (*Torah – God's teachings and way of life*) or the Prophets; I have not come to abolish them but to fulfill them. (Matthew 5:17, italics mine)

"Do not think ...." What Jesus is about to teach is apparently so new, the people might think he is doing away with the Older Testament laws. (Let's get into the practice of saying "Older Testament," not Old Testament.) But what he about to teach is not new at all. It may appear new, but only because his Jewish audience has had performance drilled into their heads for centuries.

As have we. We, can-do Americans, are all about performance, aren't we? If you think you are not, look inside a little closer. You are, at least to some degree. But your loving Heavenly Father is not looking at your performance; he is looking at your heart.

Look at these two Older Testament passages, both showing the true heart of the Father's "laws:"

> "Does the Lord delight in burnt offerings and
> sacrifices
>   as much as in obeying the Lord?

To obey is better than sacrifice,
  and to listen is better than the fat of rams.
(1 Samuel 15:22)

For I desire mercy, not sacrifice,
and to know God rather than burnt offerings. (Hosea
6:6)

Jesus repeated this "mercy over sacrifice" passage twice in his
teachings:

"But go and learn what this means: 'I desire mercy, not
sacrifice.'" (Matthew 9:13)

"If you had known what these words mean, 'I desire
mercy, not sacrifice,' you would not have condemned
the innocent." (Matthew 12:7)

He clearly wanted to get this point across. And why? Because
they – and we – had missed the true heart of the Father. The heart
behind the "laws." We must first understand the translation,
"laws," is a terrible translation. Terrible! Whenever you see "law"
think *"Torah – God's teachings and way of life."*

Yes, they carry the weight of commands, and we are to seek to
follow and obey his teachings. We all know that when we do not,
we suffer. Yet we are not so much punished for our sins as by our
sins.

If we are focused on the letter of his teachings, and not the Spirit
of his teachings, we will miss the heart of the Father, and thus live a
flat, low-energy life, with a flat, low-energy relationship with God.
Yes, he will be "God" to us, not our loving Heavenly Father. And
Jesus will be "Christ" to us, and not my Lord and Savior, and my
best friend.

The Holy Spirit through Paul put it this way:

He has made us competent as ministers of a new
covenant—not of the letter but of the Spirit; for **the**

letter kills, but **the Spirit gives life**. (2 Corinthians 3:6, bold added)

The letter kills "the life that is truly life,"[1] because we miss the Spirit, the heart and life infused throughout the Father's teachings. Instead, we focus on performance. We focus on getting it right, and not getting in trouble. That, my friend, is no life to the full.[2]

We do not want to live an "I got to" life; we want to live an "I get to" life. Next week we will discover how to do this.

---

[1] 1 Timothy 6:19
[2] John 10:10

92

The Letter Kills

Jesus told us he had not come to abolish the Older Testament, but to fulfill it.[1] He meant, in part, that he had come to fulfill the Spirit of his Father's teachings, and to move us away from legalistic rule-keeping. Jesus expressed it like this:

> The Spirit gives life; the flesh counts for nothing. The words I have spoken to you—they are full of the Spirit and life. (John 6:63)

And the Holy Spirit through Paul says,

> He has made us ... ministers of a new covenant—not of the letter but of the Spirit; for **the letter kills**, but **the Spirit gives life**. (2 Corinthians 3:6 Bold added)

So when Jesus tells his followers things like, "You think you are okay because you haven't killed anyone, but I do not want you to even carry anger in your heart," or, "You think you are okay because you have not committed adultery, but I do not what you to carry lust in your heart," he is addressing this "Letter versus Spirit" issue.[2]

The Letter of the Law is all about performance; the Spirit of the Father's teachings is all about the heart. Yes, we are to follow and obey his teachings, but not because we have to, or we are afraid of getting in trouble with God, or we want to gain his approval. That is certainly lifeless. But because we want to honor and please him.

Not we have to, but we want to.

Trying to keep the Letter of the Law is about principle-based rule-keeping. The Spirit of his teaching is prompted by a presence-based relationship.[3] Jesus' everyday presence in your life. There is no Life in rule-keeping. There is no joy in the Letter of the Law.

If you are controlled by performance, and all of us are to some degree, then you are setting yourself up for two unpleasant results. If you are really good at performance and rule-keeping, you will suffer pride and self-righteousness. If you are not so good at it, then you will suffer disappointment and despair and guilt.

I use 'suffer' purposely for both results, because not only will Jesus' Life suffer in you – in fact the Letter of Legalism will kill it – but everyone around you will suffer as well. Here is a sampling of examples of the difference between the Letter and the Spirit:

Letter vs Spirit

The Letter is about you. The Spirit is about him.

The Letter is about rules. The Spirit is about relationship.

The Letter is about, "I'll try to be good enough." The Spirit is about, "Only by His grace."

The Letter is about Willpower. The Spirit is about Joy-power.

The Letter is about Self-power. The Spirit is about Holy Spirit Power.

The Letter is about restriction. The Spirit is about freedom.

The Letter is about, "What I cannot do." The Spirit is about, "What I can do."

The Letter is about, "What I can get away with." The Spirit is about, "What I want to stay away from."

The Letter of the Law is legalistic, pedantic, and lifeless. The Spirit of Jesus' teachings, as well as the Father's teachings, are full-to-overflowing with Life. The life that is truly life.[4] And if you will free yourself from legalistic, rule-keeping performance in your life, and grasp his grace, then your life will look like:

"Streams of living water will flow from within you." (John 7:38)

---

[1] Matthew 5:17
[2] Matthew 5:21-22, 27-28 paraphrased
[3] Os Hillman
[4] 1 Timothy 6:19

93

Best is Better

At the outset of his Sermon on the Mount, Jesus tells us he has not come to abolish the Older Testament, but to fulfill it.[1] He meant, in part, that he has come to fulfill the Spirit of his Father's teachings, and to move us away from legalistic, lifeless rule-keeping, i.e. the Letter of the Law.

Last week we contrasted the Letter with the Spirit. Here are two examples:

The Letter is about, "What I cannot do." The Spirit is about, "What I can do."

The Letter is about you and your actions. The Spirit is about Jesus and your heart.

But let us go a step further. What would it look like to go far beyond the Letter of the Law – to move from Lifeless to Better, and then on to Best?

For instance, it is lifeless to think, "I got to." It is better to think, "I get to." It is best to think, "I want to."

It is lifeless to say, "I'll do my part, you do your part." It is better to say, "I'll do my part even if she/he doesn't do theirs." It is best to say, "I will proactively look for ways to serve her/him, regardless."

It is lifeless to say, "I will try not to sin." It is better to say, "I will obey my Father." It is best to say, "I want to honor and please my loving Father, who has been so gracious and good to me!"

It can be lifeless to think in terms of "God." It is better to think in terms of "Father." It is best to think in terms of "My loving Heavenly Father."

It can be lifeless to think in terms of "Christ." That is his title, by the way, not his name. It is better to call him by name, "Jesus." Perhaps it is best to think of him in terms of "My best friend." I do. Try it.

Are you stingy or greedy? Of course not! But nevertheless, it is lifeless to say, "I will give … some … when asked." It is better to say, "I will tithe to the Lord." It is best to say, "I will proactively look for ways to be generous."

Do you harbor resentment? It is lifeless to say, "I will forgive but not forget." It is better to say, I will release them and let go of this." It is best to say, "I will release and forgive, and I want to try to restore the relationship."

Do you tend to raise your voice? I'm sure not. But if so, it is lifeless to say, "I will try not to yell." It is better to say, "I will be careful with my words." It is the absolute best to say, I will be quick to listen, slow to speak and slow to become angry."[2]

'Lifeless' is playing defense. 'Better' may only be playing it safe. But 'Best' is going on offense. Best is being proactive and purposeful. Best is about taking the joy and light of Jesus to those around you with energy. Lifeless is sitting on the shore. Better may only staying in shallow water. But best is getting out there and swimming in the deep water.

Let us move beyond the lifeless life of rule-keeping. Let us be done with, "What are my boundaries? Is this a sin?" Let us move into the Life that is truly life[3] of proactive, positive, Holy Spirit energy!

Lifeless to better, and then on to best.

---

[1] Matthew 5:17
[2] James 1:19
[3] 1 Timothy 6:19

94

Lust

After Jesus drills down on anger, he starts really med-
dling when he says,

> "You have heard that it was said, 'You shall not commit
> adultery.' But I tell you that anyone who looks at a
> woman lustfully – *for the purpose of lusting* / *for the*
> *purpose of leering* / *for the purpose of fantasizing* – has
> already committed adultery with her in his
> heart. (Matthew 5:27-28 italics added)

I added the italics to give you a better sense of Jesus' meaning.
That should give many of you a sense of relief. But I plan to disrupt
that relief shortly.

I asked the men two questions as we started to study Jesus'
teaching on lust:

Can we look and not lust?

Can we look and admire and not lust?

The answer is, "Yes, absolutely." But my follow-up question
was, "And how are you doing on that?" Because, just as we can be
angry and not sin, this too is a very slippery slope. So perhaps if you
are sure you are doing fine, there might be a touch of self-delusion?

I think it is helpful to first recognize we can lust after many
things beyond just the opposite sex. Men lust after cars, pick-up
trucks, golf clubs, shotguns, just to mention a few. Ladies, you can

fill in your own list. But since Jesus ties his words to adultery, he is clearly addressing lusting after the opposite sex.

The big lie Satan uses in all cases of lust is, "That will make me happy." When he has rooted this in our heads and our hearts, our Self takes over and says next, "And I deserve it." This is then followed by, "*I have to* have it … to be happy." The Satan-hook is now in, and the reeling-in process takes over.

If you recall, we talked earlier about "Lifeless – Better – Best." Let's apply that here.

- **Lifeless:** "I will look but not lust." (If you are a man, good luck with that)

- **Better:** "I will cross the street, and/or avert my eyes, among other guardrails ."

- **Best:** To have a heart so full of "Love-Joy-Peace,"[1] that I simply have no interest in looking. I am full of love, joy and peace, because Jesus has so filled my heart. I now have an aversion to anything even close to leering.

A heart aversion to anything that will take me out of, "The flow of the Kingdom among us."[2]

So yet again, as the Master Teacher does, we start at the heart.

But the things that come out of a person's mouth come from the heart, and these defile them. 19 For out of the heart come evil thoughts—murder, adultery, sexual immorality, theft, false testimony, slander. (Matthew 15:18-19)

Lifeless – Good – Best!

John, the disciple that Jesus loved, wrote this:

There is no fear in love. But perfect love drives out fear, because fear has to do with punishment. The one who fears is not made perfect in love. (1 John 4:18)

And I add:

There is no fear, lust, anger, greed, or resentment in love. But perfect love drives out fear, lust, anger, greed and resentment. The one who fears, lusts, gets angry, is greedy, and carries resentment, is not made perfect in love.

Therefore the sure remedy for all matters of darkness in our hearts – of which lust is a charter member – is to have so much of Jesus' light and love pouring in, there is simply no room left for the rats in the cellar. This is a process, of course, and takes time. But, yes, Jesus' perfect love drives out fear, lust, anger, greed, resentment, and whatever else you have allowed to root itself into your head and heart.

We then find ourselves able to say, to anything that used to dominate us, "No thanks, I'm full." What a relief! Attractive women, or ladies, attractive men, of a certain look that used to snag you: "Yes, she/he is very attractive and all that, but no thanks, I'm full."

"Looking to lust" in our current society is the norm, but Jesus' truth is it is seedy and disgusting and nowhere near being, "In the flow of the Kingdom among us." So let us pursue purity of heart by first pursuing that ever-deepening and ever-enriching Master of our hearts, Jesus.

---

[1] Love, joy, peace, patience, kindness, goodness, faithfulness, gentleness and self-control   Galatians 5:22-23
[2] Dallas Willard

95

Capture that Thought

Previously we started to ... nervously? ... look at Jesus' words on lust:

> "You have heard that it was said, 'You shall not commit adultery.' But I tell you that anyone who looks at a woman lustfully has already committed adultery with her in his heart. (Matthew 5:27-28)

Throughout Jesus' Sermon on the Mount, he is interested in our hearts before our actions, because our actions overflow from our hearts:

> But the things that come out of a person's mouth come from the heart, and these defile them. For out of the heart come evil thoughts—murder, adultery, sexual immorality, theft, false testimony, slander. (Matthew 15:18-19)

So yet again, as the Master Teacher always does, we start at the heart:

> Above all else, guard your heart, for everything you do flows from it. (Proverbs 4:23)

How to guard our hearts – against lust, as well as anger, resentment, jealousy, greed and all the dark-heart issues so prevalent in our heads and our hearts? We must capture those thoughts before they take root in. Here is how the Holy Spirit through Paul states this:

> ... we have a divine power to demolish strongholds. 5
> ... and we take captive every thought to make it obedient to Christ. (1 Corinthians 10:4-5)

We have a divine power from the Holy Spirit to not just scratch or put a dent in those strongholds, but to actually demolish them.

Yes, take them captive! As in capture that temptation and wrestle it down and kick it out of your head before it can penetrate into your heart. Your particular temptation might be to look lustfully at the opposite sex, but it may also be the temptation to look lustfully at any number of things for which we say, "I've got to have that."

We can lust after many things beyond the opposite sex. Men lust after cars, pick-up trucks, golf clubs, shotguns, just to mention a few. Ladies, you can fill in your own list.

The big lie Satan uses in all cases of lust is, "That will make me happy." When he has rooted this in our heads and our hearts, our Self takes over and says next, "And I deserve it." This is then followed by, "*I have to* have it ... to be happy." The Satan-hook is now in, and the reeling-in process takes over.

Let's compare Adam and Eve's process to John the disciple's later words:

Genesis 3:6 the fruit of the tree was:

- good for food
- pleasing to the eye,
- desirable for gaining wisdom

1 John 2:16 For everything in the world:

- the lust of the flesh
- the lust of the eyes
- the pride of life

Eve looked at the fruit, and apparently kept looking. The temptation was setting in, and the thoughts, which she failed to capture and kick out, rolled along unabated. Perhaps her uncaptured thoughts went something like this:

"That fruit will taste good (Lust of the flesh). It sure looks pleasing (Lust of the eyes). And I am my own person, so I can make my own choices. (The pride of life) I deserve that fruit. I have to have it!"

What is the "fruit" with which you struggle? For me, many years ago when I was a hotshot, it was a 750 BMW. Or that Saddlebred horse. Or that house on Crescent Avenue. But as Jesus filled my heart over the years, I moved from, "I got to have it to be happy," to, "No thanks, I'm full."

"Yes, that is a great car. But it won't make me happy because I am already full."

Or that house, Country Club or whatever else you used to long for: "Yes, that would be fun, but I do not need it to be happy, because I am already full of joy and contentment."

Or that dress, jewelry, shoes, house, shotgun, pick-up truck, golf club: "Yes, those are all good, but I actually do not have any room left in my heart for them."

Now this, my friend, is true freedom living. Life to the full!

96

Oaths

> "Again, you have heard that it was said to the people long ago, 'Do not break your oath, but fulfill to the Lord the vows you have made.' But I tell you, do not swear an oath at all ..."
>
> —Matthew 5:33-34

Have you ever told someone you would pray for them, but forgot to? I have. Worse still, I have promised someone I would pray for them and forgot to, and they called me later to thank me for praying for them, saying, "I felt your prayers and am so grateful for you, Sam."

Jesus moves from lust, adultery and divorce – all fun topics – to "no swearing oaths." Now this seems like a misdemeanor, certainly not a felony. Who swears oaths anymore? But then he concludes with these blunt observations, which cast light on his no-oaths admonition:

> "And do not swear by your head, for you cannot make even one hair white or black. All you need to say is simply 'Yes' or 'No'; anything beyond this comes from the evil one." (Matthew 5:36-37)

Peter is the poster boy for swearing oaths about which he cannot make even one hair black or white. At the Last Supper we see Peter "Swearing to God" he will stand by Jesus,

> Peter replied, "Even if all fall away on account of you, I never will." "Truly I tell you," Jesus answered, "this very night, before the rooster crows, you will disown me three times." **35** But Peter declared, "Even if I have to die with you, I will never disown you." (Matthew 26:33-35)

A couple of hours later he cannot even stay awake while Jesus is in the midst of anguished prayer in the garden of Gethsemane, much less go to death for him:

> Then he returned to his disciples and found them sleeping. "Couldn't you men keep watch with me for one hour?" he asked Peter. (Matthew 5:40)

Do you think Jesus singled out Peter, among the three sleeping disciples, to remind Peter he should not be swearing oaths of allegiance, when he cannot even stay awake?

And a couple of hours later he is again "Swearing to God," but this time swearing he doesn't even know Jesus:

> Then he began to call down curses, and he swore to them, "I don't know the man!" (Matthew 5:74)

Now you may not find yourself in such a critical situation, but you have and you will have multiple opportunities to either, "Swear to God," or simply let your yes be yes and your no be no. The lesson we can draw from Peter's flameout is the lesson Jesus' little brother learned:

> Now listen, you who say, "Today or tomorrow we will go to this or that city, spend a year there, carry on business and make money." Why, you do not even know what will happen tomorrow. What is your life?

You are a mist that appears for a little while and then vanishes. Instead, you ought to say, "If it is the Lord's will, we will live and do this or that." As it is, you boast in your arrogant schemes. All such boasting is evil. (James 4:13-16)

I am not fond of the "If it is God's will" statement. It sounds like a cop-out. It sounds to me like you are already saying you take no responsibility for your actions. I doubt Jesus or James meant that. The point is we absolutely do want to take responsibility, and do our absolute best, "as to the Lord always," but also recognize we are human, and therefore frail and fragile, and at times selfish and myopic.

Therefore, we want to follow Jesus' counsel and not swear an oath in the first place.

Perhaps in a personal setting we could say, instead of "I promise," or "I swear I will" – something like, "I sincerely intend to carry through with my commitment. And I will. But I am human."

Or in a business situation, "You can be sure I will give this my best, and you can be sure I will in no way phone it in. You will get my best effort."

And after that, just let your "Yes be yes, and your no be no."

Part 5

Legacy

97

Letter to Finch

My daughter Britton is marrying Finch this Saturday, so if you will indulge me, I would like to vary from my usual Putting Green format and relate a personal message from my heart to Finch. (And perhaps to you, as well.)

Finch, when you have the choice of being right or being kind, choose kind, please. Being right is a withdrawal; being kind is a deposit.

View Britton in a light most favorable to her, seeing her with generous eyes, which you already do so well.

She is not as self-confident as she appears. (No one is.)

Make excuses for her in your heart, being proactive and intentional to look for the best in her.

Love her for who she is. Don't try to change her to who you want her to be.

(Allow the Holy Spirit to transform her His way.)

Don't pull out the evidence file when she errs or irritates you.

Don't try to win. In marriage, winning is losing … always—so don't try to 'checkmate' her.

You want Britton to think of you as her biggest cheerleader, not her critic.

Be sweet to her when she's not sweet.

Be kind to her when she's not kind.

Love her when she's not loveable.

When in Conflict:

Die to self. Communication won't be your biggest problem. Self will be.

Power down; don't power up.

Softer is better than louder.

Pause, listen, learn, then lead.

Finch all these things I am confident you will do well because you, my dear son, are a man after God's own heart.

And Britton, see everything above. Remember, you're too much like … me.

But, of course, as I reflect on what I have just written, this is a mirror for me, and this is a mirror for you, as well. Whether you are the husband or the wife, this is for your marriage.

Husband, treat your wife as you hope your son-in-law will treat your precious daughter.

Wife, treat your husband as you hope your daughter-in-law will treat your precious son.

I close with this joyful encouragement to Finch and Britton:

I thank my God every time I remember you. In all my prayers for both of you, I always pray with joy because of your partnership in the gospel from the first day until now, being confident of this, that he who began a good work in you will carry it on to completion until the day of Christ Jesus. And this is my prayer: that your love may abound more and more in knowledge and depth of insight, so that you may be able to discern what is best and may be pure and blameless for the day of Christ, filled with the fruit of righteousness that comes through Jesus Christ—to the glory and praise of God. (Phil. 1:1)

98

Andrew and Secundus: A Conversation

Imagine this conversation:

My little brother, Andrew, was telling us about a conversation he had with one of our more successful young converts. Secundus was Greek and was a successful trader in Roman and Greek ornaments. He was closer to Andrew's age, so he must have felt more comfortable talking to him. He started by saying, "Okay, Andrew, I'm feeling pretty good about my life. I'm starting to make some real money, so I'm thinking about things I can buy, you know, as sort of a reward for my hard work.

"I'm also looking around at what some of my friends have, and it makes me feel a little, how to say it, "competitive?" But just the other day one of my new Brothers here in Jerusalem, Amos, challenged me about being envious. He even used one of your outdated Hebrew words: "coveting."

Secundus continued, hardly catching a breath, "He even said I should think about giving money to the Lord instead of spending it all on myself. Hmp. Might I add, Andrew, Amos is a tad too legalistic for my taste?

"I'm doing alright and I've got some money to spend. As you know, it's important to look successful in my trade. Maybe I'll stretch a bit and upgrade my house and my horse, and even buy some new clothes. Even if I stretch myself a bit, I'm not worried; my income can always catch up."

But at this point he stopped and hesitated, looking down at the ground. Andrew could sense something was bothering Secundus, so he motioned to him to go on. (Andrew is a good listener. I guess he has to be with me as his bombastic big brother.)

Secundus spread his hands out palms up and said, "But I was at the morning gathering at Solomon's Porch recently, and I couldn't help but overhear two men talking. It turns out one was 70 and the other 50. They seemed engrossed in an impassioned discussion about what is really important in life."

He went on, shaking his head, "And as their conversation turned to their previous way of handling their time and their money, I could see they were disappointed with themselves. I decided to listen in for a minute. They seemed to be lamenting that they had wasted a lot of time and spent a lot of money on things that had no eternal significance."

At this Andrew broke his silence and asked Secundus, "What do you think they meant by eternal significance?"

Now Secundus became animated and exclaimed, "Eternal significance? Who thinks about that? Okay, maybe when you're 70, but at my age? Don't be ridiculous. I'm focused on how to make a living, and how to spend my time and money for the most immediate impact. Eternal significance? I've got to be thinking about now, not after I die."

Andrew was thinking to himself, "Well my friend, according to Jesus, after you die you'll be thinking a lot more about now, and how you lived your life here."

99

Andrew and Secundus' Continued Conversation

Andrew was thinking to himself, "Well my friend, according to Jesus, after you die you'll be thinking a lot more about now, and how you lived your life here." But he remained silent, which we have learned is the best response in this type of situation. Let people talk themselves out, and possibly they will hear how misguided they sound, without us having to point it out to them.

After a moment Secundus started again. "I overheard the older man say, 'I've been listening to the apostles, and it seems it really matters the way we handle our money *here*, when we get *there*.'"

The other man responded, "By there do you mean Heaven? Because I've been hearing the same thing. Perhaps it is the Holy Spirit once again giving us the clarity to hear the truth. Brother John was talking just the other day about one of Jesus' parables. It was that one about a shrewd manager who was about to get fired."

The older man broke in and said, "Yes, I do mean Heaven, and I agree, that shrewd manager story is an odd parable, for sure. When Jesus concluded his story with, 'I tell you, use worldly wealth to gain friends for yourselves, so that when it is gone, you will be welcomed into eternal dwellings,' it gave me great pause."

Secundus paused, and looked directly at Andrew, and asked, "Does he mean we should be purposeful and smart with our money, investing it in things with eternal significance? And if we do, we'll be greeted and thanked when we enter heaven by those whose lives are affected by our giving?"

"Yes, my friend, that is exactly what Jesus means," replied Andrew. "And listen to what Barnabas was teaching the other day: 'Those among us who have been blessed by the Father should seek to do good, to be rich in good deeds, and to be generous and willing to share. In this way they will lay up treasure for themselves as a firm foundation for the coming age, so that they may take hold of the life that is truly life.'"

Secundus quickly interrupted Andrew, "Jesus and Barnabas are both talking about eternal rewards, aren't they?" He paused for a moment in contemplation, then said, "Okay, so I'm listening to these two men's conversation about money and eternal significance, and I'm wanting to sluff it off and walk away, but the Holy Spirit – I guess it was Him – wouldn't let me. So I screwed up my courage and interrupted them.

"Excuse me," I said, "I couldn't help but overhear your conversation. I'm 30 and starting to make some real money. If you were me, how would you prioritize your spending and your investing?"

The 70 year old man looked me in the eye and said, "Son, do you want to be spending your money on a world that is going, or investing your money in a world that is coming?"

Andrew repeated those words, "Spending on a world going away, or investing in a world that is coming. Hmm, I like that."

Secundus frowned and said to Andrew, "Well I didn't like it. They were very nice, and sincere, but that's not really what I was looking for. "Well," I sort of stuttered in response to his question, "I'm not sure ...," but the 50 year old man interrupted me and said, "I'm curious, do you consider yourself a Christian?"

100

Planting Seeds

Do you see what God is telling us through Paul's letter to the Corinthians? I, Peter, 'the great Apostle,' may appear to be someone special. Yes, I have the strong gift of the Spirit within me. But so do you, my friend. I have healed many. I have preached mighty sermons. I have led the church. Some say I am the first Bishop.

But, and this is so important for you to understand: I am only doing my part, as the Lord has assigned to each his task. At times I plant and at times I water. He who plants and he who comes along later and waters are the same. So when you plant and when you water, you will be equally rewarded for using the gifts the Lord has given you.

If you never heal anyone, or you happen to never be present when a soul is saved, so what? Your reward is the same as mine, as you seek to promote the Kingdom. Just plant seeds. It's not complicated to plant seeds. You don't have to be a great Apostle. Just plant seeds of kindness and grace. Be casual and relaxed, yet be proactive and intentional about Jesus. He will do the heavy lifting. Since you are not responsible for anyone's salvation – thank goodness – relax and enjoy the seed-planting.

People don't care what you know until they know you care. Show them you care by establishing common ground. Invite someone to a meal. Listen to their worries. Everyone has them, you know. Be open to the interruptions – this is where ministry so often occurs.

As you cultivate common ground with a sincere heart, you will be able to season your grace with salt … with words of truth.

Do not be afraid to speak the truth. But first overwhelm them with your genuine grace. And trust me, it must be genuine.

Preach sermons all the time with grace and truth, and sometimes even use words. Anyone can plant seeds. Anyone can water them, just by being kind, just by being willing to listen. Perhaps, upon hearing someone's tale of sadness or fear, you could say, "I'll be lifting you up in my prayers." Or perhaps you could be so bold as to offer to pray with them right there on the spot.

I have found that a kind word is easy to say, and yet it often resonates in the heart for a long time as a soothing balm or even a fountain of fresh water. No sermon. No pressure. No need to bear down on anyone. But always remember this: no matter the happy front someone presents in public, no one can be truly happy without Jesus. No one. Everyone needs Jesus, they just might not see it yet.

What a joy if they saw Jesus in you, and wanted him.

I love the way Paul concluded his response to the Corinthians: "So then, no more boasting about human leaders! All things are yours, whether Paul or Apollos or Cephas or the world or life or death or the present or the future—all are yours, and you are of Christ, and Christ is of God."

Amen!

101

Staying on Track

We are all on a journey. You are hurtling at light speed into your future even as you read this. Is where you are going where you want to be when you get there? I wish I had asked that question many times in the past and changed direction accordingly. The choices we are making today, not our best intentions, determine our direction.

So, stop now and contemplate these questions: Is where I am going—in my marriage; in who or how I'm dating; in my relationships with my parents, my kids, and my friends; my drinking; my eating; my weight; my exercise (or lack thereof)—where I want to be when I arrive? Am I going to be happy with this direction later? Or, am I drifting off course?

When you were a kid at the beach with your family, perhaps you heard something like this from your parents: "You may swim in the ocean, but stay in front of the house so we can see you. Our house is green and has a South Carolina flag on the deck, so keep your eyes on it." But there was a slight current, and before I knew it, I was 10 houses down! It was only a… slight… current. I didn't even realize I had drifted so far. And now, I was in trouble.

We drift, we humans. And the problem with drifting is that it typically happens so slowly that, at first, we don't perceive where we're heading. Does anyone wake up and decide that day to have a marriage-ending affair… or, to become an alcoholic… or, to gain 30 pounds… or, to end up with a C-minus relationship with a loved one?

Does anyone wake up one day and decide to be stressed out, uptight, and not much fun to be around anymore? No, but we drift slowly, almost unperceptively, toward these things. So, we need a "green house" on the beach as a marker to keep us on course.

Oswald Chambers said,

> A Christian is someone who trusts in the knowledge and the wisdom of God, not in his own abilities. If we have a purpose of our own, it destroys the simplicity and the calm, relaxed pace which should be characteristic of the children of God.

Do you have a calm, relaxed pace, or are you hurried and harried? Notice there is a pace. I am not advocating sitting in a closet, expecting God to run your life. But, the pace is nowhere near the frenetic current of this culture… and the pace at which you may be living your life.

Remember: Satan rushes; God guides. When you have a calm, relaxed pace, you are on track. When you are hurried and harried, uptight and stressed, you are drifting way off track.

Or, how about this "marker" for relationships:

> Do nothing out of selfish ambition or vain conceit, but in humility consider others better than yourselves. (Phil. 2:3)

102

Juicy Fruit

I like to start each year grading myself on the "fruit of the Spirit": love, joy, peace, patience, kindness, goodness, faithfulness, gentleness, and self-control (Gal. 5:22-23). I put a letter-grade beside each one: A, B, C, D, or F.

How would you grade yourself on these? It's appropriate to consider because God is telling us, if we have his Spirit inside, these fruits will naturally flow from within. Most of us grade the lowest on patience and self-control. So, we mistakenly grit our teeth and make a New Year's resolution to "do better!" I like to start each year grading myself on the "fruit of the Spirit": love, joy, peace, patience, kindness, goodness, faithfulness, gentleness, and self-control (Gal. 5:22-23). I put a letter-grade beside each one: A, B, C, D, or F.

But, we don't.

God put these fruits in this order precisely because they must— they must!—grow and then flow in this order. Love is first. Try having joy without being immersed in God's love and growing in love for him? Forget it. Not going to happen. A little happiness here and there. But true joy?

And peace with no joy? Don't be silly. Patience with no peace? Absurd.

So, do you love God? Do you want to love God?

You might not. You might assume you do, but you might not.

Will you stop now and examine yourself with this blunt, objective, and honest self-evaluation: "Do I love God?"

Can you even begin to imagine the transformation? No more rules but, instead, a relationship. No longer motivated by fear but, instead, compelled by love. No more "I got to" but, instead, "I *get* to."

Don't take another step in following Jesus until you have settled the answer. It all starts here. The origin of the universe starts here. The Good News starts here. The freedom Jesus promised starts here. Your spiritual journey starts, or restarts, here.

May your desire be, each day and with each prayer, "Lord, help me to love you, and to love you more."

103

Flame Thrower

Recently, I was in a group setting with some very focused believers who I was meeting for the first time. We were challenged to ask the man seated next to us a penetrating question of some sort, so I turned and asked, "Are you a flamethrower or just a pilot light?"

He must have known exactly what I meant because he grinned and quickly responded, "I was a pilot light for too long, but lately, I've been fanning that flame into a bonfire!"

Are you confused?

God encourages us to "fan into flame" the gift of the Holy Spirit within us (2 Tim. 1:6).

We do this by living out the power of the Holy Spirit with energy, clarity, and creativity... by living life with spiritual gusto! It's not done by suppressing the fire of the Holy Spirit within us but by "making the most of every opportunity" (Eph. 5:16) to "shine the light as a lamp on a lampstand... a city on a hill" (Luke 11:33; Matt. 5:14).

When we fan into flame the power of the Holy Spirit within us, we become flamethrowers of God's warmth, power, and light.

But he also warns us not to quench this fire, not to "put out the Spirit's fire" (1 Thess. 5:19). This happens when we don't listen to the Holy Spirit's guidance and counsel, ignorantly ignoring his gentle but firm nudgings to live out the light within us.

Or, we quench by default by cramming our lives so full of noise and busyness that we cannot possibly hope to hear anything from his gentle but pervasive voice within.

In Acts 10, we find Peter up on the roof, listening, praying, and seeking God's presence. God showed up as he always will because, well, he's already there. Peter had cleared out and cleaned out enough space to be alone with God and, therefore, to be able to hear God.

The Holy Spirit suddenly spoke to Peter and told him to get outside of his comfort zone and go see Cornelius the Gentile. The Holy Spirit illustrated this by telling Peter to eat some un-kosher animals, which was anathema to good Jews.

Peter heard the Holy Spirit clearly; that's not the issue. He was thinking, "Oh, come on, God! I'm not going to do *that*! I'm not comfortable with doing this. Tell you what God, give me some more of my fellow Jews to convert. I'll jump on that."

But the Holy Spirit, in that Holy Spirit way, is persistent.

And there's the rub. Peter heard the Holy Spirit speaking to his heart, but he didn't want to do what the Holy Spirit was prodding him to do.

Can you relate? Right now, you may be uncomfortably aware of just such an incident in your life. You heard God speaking to you... clearly. There was no doubt about the message. But there was plenty of doubt about your desire to act on what you heard.

A friend related the following story to me...

"Sam, I was driving down the highway, talking on my cell with a young man I was sort of mentoring. I knew God had put me in his life to help him see Jesus. My young friend, Billy, was lamenting that, even with two jobs, he was having a hard time covering his college living expenses."

My friend then lit up and said, "I immediately heard the Holy Spirit say, 'Give him $500.' I'm telling you... it was as clear as you and I are talking now. And I was excited. Yes! That's exactly what I will do," he said, beaming. "I knew God had asked me to do it, and I was on fire to help."

Then, my friend frowned and said, "But that was in my car on the highway. By the time I got back to my office, the contest in my head had started. I pulled out my checkbook, and then, from somewhere, I suddenly felt this weight around my neck, and I thought, 'Gosh... $500 is a lot of money. Maybe just $250. That will still help him a lot.'

"But I heard God say, 'No, the amount is $500.'

"Then, I thought, 'I know what I'll do instead. I'll let my business pay for it.'"

But he looked at me and shook his head, saying, "But I heard immediately, 'No, I want *you* to pay the $500.' My next idea was to let the business pay $250, and I would pay $250. Aha! But again, that persistent voice said, 'No, I want you to pay the full $500.'"

Now, my friend was boring a hole through me with this intense look. He took a deep breath and said, "And I knew then I was just dancing with the devil. I had heard God clearly. And at first, I was on fire! I was so excited to be doing God's will. But by the time I was in the middle of the dance with the devil, I had doused my fire of excitement down to a teeny little pilot light of blasé."

We do this all the time; don't we? You have heard the Holy Spirit speaking to you. You knew exactly what He wanted you to do... or to stop doing. But then, the dialogue dance started. And you ultimately quenched the fire of the Holy Spirit and ended up back with your little C-minus pilot light.

God says, "Stop! Fan that flame into a roaring fire! *Listen* to me and then *act* on what you hear!"

A pilot light doesn't require much energy; does it? But it doesn't give off much warmth. A pilot light doesn't give off much light, either.

I'll bet there is something right now, a convicting voice saying to you, personally and individually, "You know exactly what he's talking about. You remember just recently when I put it on your heart to go see, to go help, to write that check, to call with an encouraging word, to... shine my light into that person's life."

You heard it, just as Peter did. And you wanted to act on it... at first. But then, you didn't *really* want to act on it; did you? I understand. Being a pilot light is much easier and requires much less energy than being a flamethrower.

I know a lot of pilot lights. I know plenty of quenchers. I know only a few flamethrowers. But they are oh so special. They glorify God by accurately revealing just how wonderful and powerful are the warmth, energy, and light of his Holy Spirit's fire.

You are the thermostat of your life. You can choose this day either to quench or to fan into flame the Holy Spirit's fire within you.

104

Number-One Fan

I've been thinking a lot about this idea of practicing the presence of God and how much our lives are enhanced when we *see* God all around us. He's God Almighty! He's there. I'm only encouraging you to practice... reality.

But today, I want to ask you how you think God sees *you*.

Oh, sure... He loves you. That's his job. We take for granted that he loves us because "the Bible tells me so." But if I asked you if you think God *likes* you, that's a little more iffy; isn't it? Jesus would tell you that both he and the Father like you, all the time, as well as love you.

And this motivates me to want to move closer to God. He *likes* me? He enjoys my company? Then, I want to talk with Him and to spend time with Him.

A favorite younger friend of mine lost his grandfather recently, with whom he spent a lot of time and shared a mutual feeling of affection and love. A few days later, he said this to me: "I feel like I've lost my number-one fan." That got me thinking.

What would it be about someone such that you would feel that person is your number-one fan? Maybe that person always sees the best in you? Maybe he or she is loyal and devoted to you regardless of your behavior? When someone accuses you or places you in a bad light, your number-one fan not only cannot imagine what that person is talking about, but he or she would defend you always.

That person sees everything about you in a light most favorable to you and is always on your side. He or she enjoys spending time with you... just to be around you.

That person roots for you, cheers you on, and encourages you constantly.

A number-one fan wants the best for you, sees only the best in you, and always assumes the best about you.

Do you have a number-one fan? Maybe your mother or your father? Your children (assuming they're not teenagers) or your grandchildren?

May I suggest who your true number-one fan is? Your God and his Son, Jesus. Just read these previous descriptions; this is them! They adore you. They are on your side. They always want the best for you, and they love for you to be with them.

They think you are great, even when you obviously are not.

Jesus actually calls us friends and describes God as a loving Father who, when He sees us turn back toward him, kicks off a huge celebration, throws a party, and rushes out to greet us, shushing us as we start to offer our apologies for straying from and stiff-arming him.

He's not angry. He doesn't require us to grovel. There is no grudge held, even when we might deserve it.

"No. Hush," he says. "Don't say another word. You're back. That's all that matters. I've never stopped loving you... or *liking* you for that matter. Come on in. Take my best robe. You're back where you belong. Start the feast and let's celebrate!" (Luke 15:11; paraphrase from *The Prodigal God* by Tim Keller)

And when you get this... when you see this is how God sees you, your heart will fill up with his love, and in a wonderful reversal, you will become *his* number-one fan. Then, you will see God always in the best light. You will always be ready to defend him, to believe the best about him, to trust him, and... you'll want to spend more and more time with him.

May you learn to see God as he sees you... and to become his number-one fan as he is yours.

105

Bumping the Trajectory

I love to hike to the top of Tablerock. It is 3.6 miles to the top with a vertical climb of 2,000 feet. Not so easy. Along the way, there are several rock plateaus that afford beautiful views, and one could stop there and still enjoy the... partial... climb.

But you won't see the view from the top. And you won't know what you are missing.

I have watched groups start with the fixings for the picnic they think they are going to have at the top: folding chairs, picnic baskets, and even a boom box. And I've watched those same groups who, after an hour or so of climbing, realize they have a decision to make. They will either settle for less by stopping at a lower plateau, or they will shed some of their stuff to go higher. They can't hold onto all of their things and still go for the top.

Most settle for the lower plateaus and never know what they're missing.

Once we get off the broad road to destruction and enter through this narrow gate, we're on the adventure of a lifetime! We're growing spiritually, our enthusiasm is energized, and we feel so close to the Lord. Jesus is now our friend as well as our Savior, and we feel the difference in our hearts.

But... after a while, we plateau. We flatten out. "What happened to my enthusiasm? I was on such a high. Now, I feel like I'm drifting... sort of aimlessly. And I don't like it."

We all plateau. So we have to do things differently.

The mantra for fitness is "muscle confusion." We can't keep doing the same exercises week after week and expect to advance. We will plateau. And isn't this true in our marriages? Ever been in a rut? And it's true in all areas throughout our lives.

To get out of the rut, off our plateau, and moving onward and upward again, we must "bump the trajectory," typically by shedding whatever is holding us back.

If you want things to be different, you have to do things differently.

Now, the real question is this: Are you satisfied with your spiritual life, or do you want things to be different? I know. I know... It sounds like a trick question. No one should ever be satisfied to the point of complacency, yet it is a wonderful place to be comfortable and confident in your relationship with the Lord.

But I'm asking if your spiritual journey has flattened out. Or, I guess I'm asking if you even care enough to consider it a journey with a desire to be making progress. Perhaps you're comfortable with your weekly routine: church on Sunday and possibly a little *extra* here and there.

Jesus wants you to keep advancing. He knows what you are missing. So he invites you to drop whatever may be holding you back and to come closer and go deeper:

> Then he said to them all: "If anyone would come after
> me, he must deny himself and take up his cross daily
> and follow me." (Luke 9:23-25)

If you want the top of Tablerock, you'll have to deny yourself some things.

Eugene Peterson tells of a time when he visited a monastery, and at the welcome meeting, the speaker said, "If you realize you forgot something you can't live without, see one of the monks, and he'll show you how to."

Jesus says, "*If* you want this, come on, and follow me. But I'm going to the top, so be prepared to let go of a few things on the way. You won't be able to save for yourself all the things you *think you must have* to be happy. I'll show you how to let go of (lose) those things and find the life that is truly life."

This is what Jesus meant by, "For whoever wants to save his life will lose it, but whoever loses his life for me will save it."

Are you settling for less? Are you satisfied with the lower plateau? You'll possibly achieve a semblance of a good life. But you will never know what you're missing.

Or are you willing? Do you *want* to advance toward the top? You will never regret it. It is so worth the effort. It is immeasurably, abundantly more than anything you could ask or even imagine to ask for (see Eph. 3:22-24).

106

Change: The Baptism of Repentance

As we began 721 Ministries several years ago, I thought I would encounter opposition from intellectualism, skepticism, or outright disbelief. But, as of late, I have realized my adversary is often change... change for the better but not transformation for the best. Here is a typical encounter:

> I was achieving all of my goals. I had the wife and kids, a big house, and was on the way to a bigger one. But as I got into my 40s and 50s, I realized there had to be more to life. This couldn't be all there was. So I got real involved at church and a men's group, and now, I feel so much better. I've really changed for the better.

Or...

> I got into my 40s and 50s and went through a divorce, an illness, and a financial crisis, and I realized there had to be more to life. So, I got real involved at church and a women's group, and I now feel so much better. I've really changed for the better.

And my favorite...

As I've gotten older, I've changed. I've mellowed. I've lost interest in all those old habits. (In other words, "I'm not really any better or holier. I'm just too tired to sin anymore.")

The common theme is this:

The way I was wasn't working, so I changed direction. I quit… or, cut back on [come on… even moderation in moderation] the things that were creating problems in my life.

These folks—and you, maybe—experienced what God calls the "baptism of repentance." *Repent* means "to change direction," and that is exactly what they did. And they did it well. They got involved at church. They got better. Things got better. Can you relate to this?

But change will only get you better. Transformation is the key to the best… the Holy Spirit's best.

You can do change in your own power. You can't do transformation at all. True transformation is what the Holy Spirit does to you… in you. Living with the power of the Holy Spirit is transformational. It can take you from the C-minus life to the A-plus life.

This is why the story in Acts 19 is so important:

As Paul entered Ephesus he met twelve men who looked like disciples of Jesus. They were dressed nicely and were just leaving a Bible Study. Paul asked them if they were believers and they responded with a resounding, "Of course!" But he then asked them, "Did you receive the Holy Spirit when you believed? Did you take God into your mind only, or did you also embrace him with your heart? Did he get inside you?" "We've never even heard of that—a Holy Spirit? God within us? No, we were baptized in John's baptism. And since then we have really changed a lot. It's been so great." "That explains it," said Paul. "John preached a baptism of repentance, of radical life-change. You've only had a change, but not a radical one. You'll need the Holy Spirit to be transformed into a new person, not just a changed person." (Acts 19:1-4, MSG, paraphrased by Sam)

As I get older, I'm feeling much more like Ward Cleaver than Mel Gibson. I've changed a lot since my earlier days. But some of this change has just made me older... not necessarily holier. This is true for many of us. We've learned the hard way what we don't want to do or to be. As it has been said, "Good judgment comes from experience. Experience comes from bad judgment."

But that's all about change, and change will only take me so far. I need more. I need help. I need the Holy Spirit. The baptism of repentance is this: "God, I want things to change, so I'll change... some." The baptism of the Holy Spirit is this: "Father, I want to be more than just changed; I want to be transformed into a different person... a new creation!"

If you're not as wild, stupid, loud-mouthed, argumentative, drunk, or whatever as you used to be, you've stepped up from a C-minus to a C-plus. That's better. But if you want the best, ask for the Holy Spirit. Then, start asking for him to transform you into the A-plus-life-that-is-truly-life kind of person he created you to be.

107

Spectator: Getting into the Game

We all know college football is a passion across the country, and perhaps no conference more intense than the Southeastern Conference (SEC). I love college football, too, but I'm not really passionate about any particular team. I'm more of a spectator. And even though the SEC fans are not actually out on the field playing, their passion, involvement, and heartfelt commitment goes far beyond being a mere spectator like me.

I'm well-meaning, enjoy the games, and watch many of them, but my heart is not invested.

In the *Book of Acts*, Paul came upon a group of seemingly dedicated followers of Jesus. They must have proclaimed to be followers of Jesus, and I'm guessing they looked the part. After all, they were called "disciples." But the story took an odd twist. Listen to the dialogue:

> Now, it happened that while Apollos was away in Corinth, Paul made his way down through the mountains, came to Ephesus, and happened on some disciples there. The first thing he said was, "Did you receive the Holy Spirit when you believed? Did you take God into your mind only, or did you also embrace him with your heart? Did he get inside you?"

"We've never even heard of that—a Holy Spirit? God within us?"

"How were you baptized, then?" asked Paul.

"In John's baptism."

"That explains it," said Paul. "John preached a baptism of radical life-change so that people would be ready to receive the One coming after him, who turned out to be Jesus. If you've been baptized in John's baptism, you're ready now for the real thing, for Jesus." (Acts 19:1-4, MSG)

At a men's gathering to explore questions about the Bible, the ice-breaker question is often, "Tell us where you are in your spiritual journey, using football as an analogy." The answers can be poignant, revealing, and downright funny.

- "I'm on the team, but I'm on the sidelines."

- "I'm on the team, but I'm playing more defense than offense."

- "I'm on the team, but I'm getting too many penalties."

- "I'm on the team, but I need to study the playbook more so I can get back in the game."

- "I think I'm on the team, but most of the time, I feel like a spectator sitting in the stands."

- "I'm not just a spectator in the stands… I'm sitting at home on the sofa with chips and crumbs on my shirt."

One night, we had this response: "I'm outside the stadium, trying to find the door in."

The next day, this man called me to say he was experiencing a heart change and an eye-opening awakening unlike anything he had experienced before. I could sense something big was changing in his life; and trust me… it stuck. My new friend retooled his life's direction (repented) and began a heartfelt and compelling pursuit of Jesus.

One day, this friend said to me, "You know... almost one year before that night when I said I was outside the stadium looking for an entrance, I had actually prayed the sinner's prayer with sincerity, asking the Lord to come into my heart. I was very sincere, and it was heartfelt. I was sure I was saved then. Except... I wasn't so sure. Nothing had really changed in my life, but now a year later, the day after that night with you guys, Jesus really lit me up, and I could see for the first time how blind I had been and how much I had missed it. What happened? What's the difference between a year ago, praying the sinner's prayer, and..." He hesitated, grappling for the right word. "And... *this*?"

My answer? A year ago, he wanted to change and sincerely so. As a result, he was "baptized" with John's "baptism of repentance." He was already well-respected in the community and had been attending church irregularly. He was trying to pray a little more, give a little more, and read his Bible... a little more.

He knew more *about* Jesus, but he didn't know Jesus.

There was no baptism of the Holy Spirit.

And this is where I want you to do a self-check.

I know this will offend many, but from my observation, the *vast* majority of people in church, well-meaning and sincere people, have only experienced "John's baptism." These folks, perhaps you included, are far beyond me morally and have much better life track records than I.

But... You must confront yourself, and answer the question, "Did you take God into your mind only, or did you also embrace him with your heart? Did he get inside you?"

Are you a mere spectator (most of you are, though well-meaning and sincere)?

If you've been baptized in John's baptism but haven't experienced the baptism of the Holy Spirit, are you ready now for the real thing? For Jesus?

A follow-up note: To clarify, this baptism of the Holy Spirit is not merely a "speaking-in-tongues" event, and it is not a "falling-down-and-flopping-around" event. It is simply the Holy Spirit moving into your heart because you have finally realized you have missed it and are fully engaged in surrender to Jesus as your new King and your absolute Savior. Something shifts inside, and you know you will never be the same. The light comes on, and the simple explanation is that "all I know is I was blind but now I see."

108

Drifting and Plateauing

One thing I know about us humans is that we drift. We drift in our relationships, our careers, our exercise, and much more: "It's been three weeks… months… years… since I _____ " – and you easily can fill in the blank, I'm sure.

We drift in our weight: "I gained 10 pounds! Where did that come from?" We drift in our Bible reading, in our staying in touch with others, and in how many other ways?

And in all these areas, we will plateau, as well. We stop growing. We coast.

You drift. I drift. But don't miss this: no one drifts *toward* the A-plus life to the full.

And, no matter our self-discipline or our drive, we will plateau. We will flatten out, get bored, or just lose our mojo.

Drifting and plateauing: a C- life for sure.

So we must be intentional about making periodic course corrections.

We are all on a journey. As you read this, you are hurtling at light speed along your future. The show-stopping question is this: "Is where you're going where you want to be when you get there?" (Andy Stanley) In my line of work, I constantly see the results of ignoring this question: relationship debris and emotional shrapnel scattered everywhere. I'm often tempted to ask, "Did you not see that coming?" But then, I would first have to turn the mirror back on myself.

The remedy is to continue to take stock of our direction and make periodic course corrections to stop the drifting. Of course you've already tried to do this many times … in your own power… with the results being less than dazzling. Maybe you made some progress, only to flatten out again and plateau.

You may have even tried something radical like the "Sinner's Prayer" for a major course correction. But it was for self-improvement, not surrender to the King. The Holy Spirit likely didn't really get inside you.

Jesus had something to say about our need for these course corrections. He knows all too well about our drifting and plateauing, and he knows all too well about where we can end up if we don't make the necessary course corrections. Jesus warned we are all drifting along the highway to destruction and we must change course. He alerts us to this danger with these words:

> "Enter through the narrow gate. For wide is the gate and broad is the road that leads to destruction, and many enter through it. But small is the gate and narrow the road that leads to life, and only a few find it." (Matt. 7:13-14)

Only a few?

So Jesus sets out a course correction for us: the narrow gate. Have you entered through it? Are you sure?

109

95%—Are You Offended?

I may have shocked many with this statement:

I live in the South. It is where I joyfully live and move
and have my being. Just about everyone I know here
believes Jesus is the Son of God. And about 95% of them
are going to Hell.

If I offended, you please know you would be offended by Jesus
as well. He said it first. I am only putting a quantity to his blunt
statement:

"Then Jesus went through the towns and villages,
teaching as he made his way to Jerusalem. Someone
asked him, "Lord, are only a few people going to be
saved?"

His answer: "Only a few." (Luke 13:22-30 and Matthew 7:13-
14)

Perhaps read them both?

"Only a few" lines up with my observations over these past 22
years. We started 721 Ministries because we felt compelled to pro-
claim Jesus' warnings in the above passages. Before 721's inception,
I was teaching young adult Sunday School classes every Sunday at
15 different churches around South Carolina.

The couples in attendance were all really nice "Christian" men
and women. The ladies were for the most part tuned in, listening

and some even taking notes. The men? Not so much. They were bored, distracted by all the details of their busy lives swirling around in their heads.

Only they were not Christians; they were Churchians. They were not following Christ; they were following church.

They did not come to Sunday School to get a lecture from me about pursuing Jesus – they came because it was what they were supposed to do. It was Sunday morning in the South. You go to church. If you have children, you get them to Sunday School, so you might as well go, too. What would your friends think of you if you didn't?

My heart cried out inside. These men were doing what they thought they were supposed to be doing. No one was telling them "there's more." They were the audience Jesus was warning in the above Luke and Matthew passages.

One Sunday morning I was teaching the 'grown-ups' class at a church: the elders and deacons and older patriarchs and matriarchs of this church. I explained what I did in last week's Putting Green: that "believe" in the Scriptures actually means so much more than simply accepting as true a set of facts about Jesus.

A 75-year-old friend approached me after the class – he actually chased me down, somewhat breathlessly. He exclaimed, "I've never heard anything like that before. I've been in this church my entire life. I have based my salvation on the Romans 10:9 passage:

> "If you declare with your mouth, 'Jesus is Lord,' and believe in your heart that God raised him from the dead, you will be saved."

"Are you telling me I'm missing it?"

After that day, and for years later, this friend, his name was Sam also, said to me, "I was on a fast track to Hell, and I didn't have a clue. No one had ever told me there was more to "believe" than just believe. I thank the Lord daily that someone was willing to offend an entire Sunday School class so I could hear the true Gospel."

Please, I take no pleasure in offending anyone, but do please hear this: If I offended you last week, you are quite likely in the same place as my friend Sam was.

Will you set aside your offense and surrender to Jesus?

110

Babble on in Babylon

For the past several weeks the 721 groups have been studying the book of Daniel.

Beth Moore has a series on Daniel and in one of her sessions she read the poem below. It is written by a woman for women. I decided to adopt it in a version for men.

Below are both.

Enjoy – and be convicted!

Babble on in Babylon (For Women)

Brimming closets, shoe racks bulge, one in every color,
    I'll just indulge.
My wildest whim will oft be met, bigger, faster, give
    me, get.
Travel on in Babylon.

May I go first? Knew you'd not care, for my time's
    precious. You've lots to spare.
I'll slip in front and off I'll go. See, I'm quite fast and
    well, you're quite slow.
I and me fast friends, life-long.
    Prattle on in Babylon.

(Nip it here, just there a lift. I just turned forty, it was a
    gift.

The eyes, the lips, the bosoms do, sculptured, lasered,
    injected, too.
No wrinkles left, the tummy's gone.
Journey on in Babylon.)

Enough of me, how do you view me?
You get one, but give me three.
I couldn't bare to just say no, it's my desire and rightly
    so.
Add another and on and on.
Shuffle on in Babylon.

No end in sight that I can see, today is blocked by the
    mirror in front of me.
A wreck, a death, tsunami tide, it mildly stirs me, I
    must confide.
TV claims tens of thousands gone.
Oh well, let's see what else is on.
Numb to the stunning sight of each new dawn,
Sinking fast in Babylon.

Like a lobster in a pot who begins to like the water
    hot,
I've been duped, been tricked, been had, convinced
    that truth was somehow bad.
Evil, coddled and cooed and purred, and beckoned
    me and called and lured.
Now in a place with the lights turned on, I'm racing
    home from Babylon.
I'm racing home from Babylon.

    – Lynn Parker

Babble on in Babylon (For Men)

My rep is so important, my wallet therefore must
    bulge. I'll take one in every color, I must indulge.

My wildest whim must be met, bigger, faster, give me,
  get.
I deserve it, don't you see. From day one, it's all about
  me.
Travel on in Babylon.

May I go first? Knew you'd not care, for my time's
  precious. You've lots to spare.
I'll slip in front and off I'll go. See, I'm quite fast and
  well, you're quite slow.

"I and me" such fast friends, life-long.
Prattle on in Babylon.

I did it my way, I did a lot. I want it, I need it, I'm after
  the pot.
Work harder, stay longer. My family will understand
  one day,
Why I insisted I do it my way.
Journey on in Babylon

Enough of me, how do you view me?
You get one, but give me three.
I couldn't bare to just say no, it's my desire and rightly
  so.
Add another, I need more, and on and on.
Shuffle on in Babylon.

No end in sight that I can see, today is blocked by the
  mirror in front of me.
I see me, so I don't see you. There's just so much I
  need to do.
I'm so busy, I'm so distracted, I've lost my focus,
The things truly important seems like hocus-pocus.
I'm numb to the sight of each new dawn.
Sinking fast in Babylon.

Like a lobster in a pot who begins to like the water
    hot,
I've been duped, I've been tricked, I've been had; I
    was convinced that truth was somehow bad.
Evil, coddled and cooed and purred, and beckoned
    me and called and lured.
But now I'm exposed, with the lights turned on, so I'm
    racing home from Babylon.
I'm racing home from Babylon.

    – Lynn Parker and Sam Hunter

111

A Personal Letter

I want to encourage you to start reading the scriptures again, or more often, or with more depth. My motivation is similar to telling you about a great movie. I want you to experience what I have experienced—the joy and the richness of reading a personal love letter from God Almighty, creator of the universe.

If the Bible is anything but this for you, then I want to create a shift in your perspective of, attitude about, or even your understanding of God's word. Perhaps it appears pedantic and stiff and not very relational. I understand. But it is not; it is so much more.

To help with a perspective shift, let me give you a living, breathing example.

When I was fifteen, I attended a basketball camp, the largest basketball camp in the country, at Campbell College in North Carolina. John Wooden of UCLA fame was there, and I was in a group session with him one entire morning. Coach Wooden was a basketball god—not to be sacrilegious, but he was.

Yet the ultimate experience was a small group of us spending an hour or so with Pete Maravich. He was my idol! Just look him up on YouTube for his basketball wizardry. Pete taught me—me personally, me Sam—how to spin a basketball on my fingers, as well as several other tricks.

I treasured his tricks in my heart for years, and practiced them over and over—at the gym, around the house. Just ask my mother about all the broken lamps.

Now suppose Pete Maravich had pulled me aside and said, "Sam, I want you to experience the fullness of basketball, and all that this basketball life has to offer, so I am going to write down all my thoughts, my teachings, my philosophy on basketball, everything I have in my heart and in my head, and I am going to send it all to you in a long letter."

Picture the day I received this basketball bible from my hero. Would I think to myself, "Oh my, I can't believe I have to read all this? What a drudgery. I don't have time for this. And anyway, there is nothing in here that really speaks or applies to me. I think I will instead read the newspaper, or flip through a magazine, or watch some TV—or whatever."

No, I wouldn't think that! I can only imagine the joy I would experience as I opened his letter, seeking to learn and absorb everything in it.

God Almighty, the creator of the heavens and the earth, has put in writing, "All My thoughts, My teachings, My philosophy on life, everything I have in My heart and My head, and I am sending it all to you."

And please do not miss this: to you, personally. Yes, it is for everyone, but it is also to you, and for you, my friend.

Perhaps try again reading his very personal letter to you in this new light. There is a richness awaiting you. And Jesus is there to meet you as you open the scriptures to your newly opened heart.

112

Invite—Involve

"If you want things to be different you have to do things differently."

Do you want things to be different? Do you want to keep growing – in all areas of your life – or are you satisfied just coasting? I am frequently looking for ways to bump my trajectory, especially in my walk with Jesus. I use the word "walk" intentionally, because walking is the measure of a life of faith.

The Holy Spirit prompted the prophet Isaiah to write:

> Even youths grow tired and weary, and young men stumble and fall; but those who hope in the Lord will renew their strength. They will soar on wings like eagles; they will run and not grow weary, they will walk and not be faint. (Isa. 40:30-31)

"... they will walk and not be faint."

When I am soaring with emotion on a spiritual high my focus and my devotion to Jesus can be easy. And, I like running because it feeds my inner achievement drive. But to walk, calmly, quietly and constantly with Jesus? This is not so easy, is it? I like movement, I like motion, I like measurable mountains!

But this is not the way of the disciple of Jesus. This is:

> When Christ's abiding presence becomes our guide, then guidance becomes an almost unconscious

response to the gentle moving of His Holy Spirit within us. (Bob Mumford, *Take Another Look at Guidance*)

"The gentle moving of His Holy Spirit within us." But how to live this?

May I suggest you adopt this practice: **Outset – Reset?**

At the outset of each day invite Jesus into your day. Invite him into the details of your day. In the morning I look over my Daytimer and the list of things to do, and I invite Jesus into each meeting, each errand, each task.

Jesus makes a rather remarkable promise about this **Outset: Invite**:

> Here I am! I stand at the door and knock. If anyone
> hears my voice and opens the door, I will come in and
> eat with that person, and they with me.
> (Rev. 3:20)

Are we to take Jesus literally? Is it that simple? I just open the door of my heart and in he comes?

Yes.

But you must mean it and you must want it. Perhaps your prayer may just be, "Jesus help me to want to want to invite you in." He knows your heart. He is not expecting you to be perfect – even in your "wanting." You open the door of your heart; he will take care of the coming in part.

This is a wonderful start to your day. If you start this practice – and it will take practice – it will change your day. And it will change ... transform ... you.

113

What Will Be Your Story?

1. *Are you worried; are you hurried?*
2. *What are you learning; what are you changing?*
3. *What will be your story after this?*
   a. *Irritation or transformation?*
   b. *White knuckling or white funerals?*
   c. *Getting through it or going deeper?*

What will be your story after this C-19 time?

Hear me clearly on this: You will have a story to tell in the years to come. You will be telling your children and your grandchildren about this time.

What will be your story?

Will it be all about your irritation, or about life changes that led to transformation?

Will you talk about how you white-knuckled your way through this, saying something like, "It wasn't easy, but got through it?"

Or will you be able to talk about letting go, loosening your grip on your worried and hurried life?

Permanent Change Leads to Transformation

My parents, as many of yours, lived through the Great Depression, as well as WWII. They were influenced by these two experiences for the rest of their lives.

On a light note, my 95-year-old mother still craves syrup. When she orders pancakes or waffles, she practically drowns them in syrup. And each time she will look up and smile sheepishly and say, "Syrup was rationed during WWII. If we got any at all, it was a thimble full. Ever since, I can never get enough."

I love when this happens (at least a thousand times), because I get to see that young teenage girl in her eyes.

But more significantly were the life-long transformations her generation experienced. These children of the Depression took nothing for granted. They were conservative with their money and their resources, wasting nothing.

My parents would drive me nuts with their 1/3 bananas and 1/2 apples browning up in the frig. They would keep leftovers that would barely feed a squirrel. Going out to restaurants was a rare treat. They would be just as happy, no, *much more* happy staying at home.

They were conservative with their money, and yet generous and eager to invest in their community, their church, and those in need. They became the greatest generation ever, and the millionaires next door.

These changes brought about from their experience with the Great Depression and WWII became permanent changes, transforming the rest of their lives. And do not miss this: they never drifted from these core values of honesty, hard work, decency, and integrity.

The culture held no sway over them. Their generation enjoyed the simpler life, rarely distracted by the nonsense – the absolute nonsense – by which we are all so easily distracted – and worried and hurried.

These folks had experienced two "plate-tectonic shifts" in their lives, and they were deeply transformed by them – for not just the better, for the best.

Will you be?

What will be your story about this C-19 time, as you go about the rest of your life? Will it be about toilet paper or transformation?

114

Living from the Grave Backwards

What will people say to your children and your family about you at the reception after your funeral? Now is the time to live what you would want them to say.

Let's put it another way: What would you want to say if you had a chance to give a farewell speech before you die? Now is the time to write it—by the way you live day to day.

Older age, getting closer to the end, brings with it an acute perspective about what is and what is not important. Solomon lost this perspective at some point, and obviously missed the most important things:

> "Meaningless, meaningless," says the Teacher. "Utterly meaningless! Everything is meaningless." (Ecc. 1:2)

Stop for a moment and picture you exclaiming this at your farewell speech.

I have stood at the graveside of my father, and of two close friends. As I stood there each time, I reflected on their life, and our life together. I could not help but ponder the things I wish I had said to them, and the things I wish I had done with them, or for them. I also pondered the things I wish I had not said, and the things I wish I had not done.

I think I regret what I did not do or say much more.

But it has occurred to me, to avoid such regret, or at least to minimize it, perhaps I could think about my own grave, or my own farewell speech, and start to live backwards from there. This is not a pessimistic approach; it is a proactive approach.

Two stories to illustrate.

My friend's father, Bill, is a very nice man. He is a successful businessman, but maybe not the warmest man in the room. Nice, kind, not cold—just not particularly warm. I was around many times when Bill's mother came around. She was invited to all the holidays, some birthdays, but fewer just-casual gatherings.

She was a tad abrasive, but Bill tolerated her, and was generally kind to her.

After his mother died, Bill uncharacteristically sobbed on and off for 3 days. He would be standing in the kitchen, drinking a breakfast cup of coffee, and suddenly he would break down in sobs.

He was not a neglectful son to his mother, just not a doting, loving son.

And now he was paying for it.

My friend Ford had two daughters. He would often brag on Sissie. Sissie was a model child. She made fine grades, was respectful to Ford, and loving. She was his pride and joy. But his daughter Maggie gave him fits for years. She was not just rebellious; she was a hellion. She ran away, she stole from Ford and his wife, and even his elderly mother. She cursed them all when confronted.

Ford died at a relatively young age. At his funeral, when the family entered from the side door, one daughter was controlled and together. The other was sobbing so hard her whole body shook. She could hardly walk she was so distraught, clinging on to her sister, her body racking with pain.

Which daughter do you think she was?

The young wayward daughter and the adult, not-doting son were both filled with regret and remorse. But this does not have to be you. You can affect this now. And now, by the way, is the only time you can affect it.

Solomon gave us a warning about this in his own "Farewell speech":

Yet when I surveyed all that my hands had done and what I had toiled to achieve, everything was meaningless, a chasing after the wind; nothing was gained under the sun. (Ecc. 2:11)

I will not chase after the wind anymore. I do not want to stand over anymore graves, or contemplate my own, with any thoughts of regret and remorse. I plan to think about my farewell speech, and not write it now, but live it now.

I want to think about the eternal nature of everything I do, because now, right now as you read this, is the first minute of your eternity. And eternity is a long time.

115

A Simple Yes No

"And do not swear by your head, for you cannot make even one hair white or black. All you need to say is simply 'Yes' or 'No'; anything beyond this comes from the evil one."

—Matthew 5:36-37

Jesus uncovers something deep within us when he

warns us "… anything beyond this comes from the evil one."Let's first establish Jesus is not advocating a literal "Yes" or "No," but instead a simple, straightforward and to-the-point response. With no blabbering on afterward.

But what is it in us that compels us to say more than a simple, straightforward answer? Insecurity? A need to convince others of our integrity? A need to get our way?

Jesus' admonition reminds me of my father's generation. I am sure I never heard my father, or anyone else from his generation ever say, "I swear to God." Or, "I promise you I'm telling the truth." And why? There was no need. Their word was their bond, and everyone knew it.

Picture a man or woman in a small town being called as a witness in a trial. They lay their hand on the Bible to swear to tell the truth and the judge stops them. "I know you. There is no need to have you swear to tell the truth. You always do, and everyone knows it."

Would it be this could always be said about each of us?

So right away we start to see Jesus is addressing our hearts, and perhaps our own perceived lack of integrity. I know in my heart I am not totally trustworthy, so I feel compelled to assure you I am. I am not dishonest; I am human. Do we always tell the truth, the whole truth, and nothing but the truth?

No.

At times we manipulate the "truth" to either cover our short-comings or to get our way. And now we see the next reason Jesus stated, "...anything beyond this comes from the evil one." When I shade the truth, or tell what I consider to be white lies, I may be doing so to simply hide my human faults. But I am often doing so to get my way. I know how to arrange my words so as to sway you to my side, or to my way of doing things.

I would never call it manipulating (because that would be from the evil one). But who am I kidding? It is certainly not "Walking in the light."[1]

In my early twenties, I worked for the Republican National Committee. They taught us a simple yes-no answer that has stuck with me over these forty years: "When your candidate is accused of some nefarious action, have them reply with one of these three responses, and not word more:

1. "No I did not do it." (Period)

2. "Yes I did do it and I am sorry. I was wrong. I hope you will forgive me." (Period)

3. "Yes I did it and I would do it again. I believe what I did was right, necessary, and appropriate." (Period)

Do you remember Senator Larry Craig, the man arrested for "tapping his foot" in the men's restroom, as a signal to invite activity with another gay man? His explanation of "having a wide stance" when he sat down was utterly ridiculous. He looked like a fool blabbering on. He would have been much better off employing one of the above three.

If Richard Nixon had employed the second response, the country would have forgiven him and there would be no Watergate scandal. And the same with Bill Clinton, and his silly definition of "is."

We know when we are going beyond a simple yes or no. Our emotions are kicking in, and our heart rate is pumping up, even if just a little. The next time you hear yourself going beyond a simple, straightforward response, perhaps picture Satan sitting on your shoulder, and remember Jesus' words, and know exactly where it is coming from.

---

[1] 1 John 1:7-9

116

Who Are You?

We finished 2021, pre-Christmas, studying the Beati-
tudes. I intend to return to the Beatitudes for a thorough deep dive.
But for now, I want to start this new year reminding you of "What
is most Important."

Here again is a short story about a rabbi and his encounter with
a Roman soldier.[1]

It seems our rabbi takes the wrong fork in a road on his way
home one night, and soon thereafter he is startled by a shout: "Who
are you? What are you doing here?"

The rabbi realizes he has stumbled upon a Roman outpost and
for a moment he freezes in his steps. Again, the Roman soldier roars,
"Who are you? What are you doing here?"

The rabbi pauses for a moment, and then he calls out, "How
much do you get paid a day?" Perplexed by the rabbi's response,
the solder replies, "I get paid two denarii a day, Jew. Why?"

The rabbi responds, "Because I will double your wage if you
come to my house every morning and ask me those same two questions."

Oh my.

So I ask you, *you*, "Who are you? What are you doing here?"

These two questions are tightly linked together, because the
way you answer the second, answers the first. Put another way,
what I am about each day, my to-do list, my order of priorities, becomes who I am.

Can I get you to picture yourself leaving the house in the morning, already distracted and a possibly a tad frayed. And standing in front of you is someone who stops you and asks,

Who are you?

What are you doing here?

How would you answer these two questions?

"Uh, I'm just trying to get through the day. I'm already backed up and I've got texts and emails pinging as we speak. Would you just leave me alone!"

Or more poignantly, how would others?

"He/she is … a successful lawyer, doctor, business person, teacher. Really smart. Really driven. Drinks a little too much. A fun friend. A really good golfer, tennis player, hunter, fisherman, poker player, designer. A huge Clemson or Carolina fan. Loves a good party."

Or, "He/she made a difference in my life." – "He/she knows Jesus." – "There is something different, deeper, about him/her. I want what they have."

The rabbi wants the soldier to come each morning to remind him to think deeply about his answers before he starts his day, because he understands that each day becomes each month, becomes each year, become his life … his legacy.

Remember, inheritance is what you leave for someone; legacy is what you leave in someone.

Who are you?

What are you doing here?

---

[1] *Make Your Mark* by Brad Gray

117

Who is Jesus?

C.S. Lewis and J.R.R. Tolkien were close friends, both
with absolutely brilliant minds, and the ability to make seemingly
complicated theology very simple. Lewis famously observed, "Jesus
is either who he said he is, or he is a liar or a lunatic. He did not
leave us any other options. He did not intend to."[1]

When I was reading Mere Christianity in June of 1995 and came
to this statement, the Light came on, and my life changed forever. I
did not realize it at the time, but I was born again. I remember thinking, with sudden and total clarity, "It is true! Jesus did walk on this
earth, and he was God incarnate. He was the Son of God, and I must
change everything about my life and pursue him with everything I
have."

J.R.R. Tolkien, as he was seeking to convince Lewis to take
Christianity seriously, stated, "Christianity is either of ultimate importance, or it is not important at all. But one thing it is never, and
can never be, is kind of important."[2]

Is he right?

Last week we started 2022 with two questions:

1. Who are you?
2. What are you doing here?

Today let's ask these questions:

1. Who is Jesus?

2. If he is who he said he is, then what am I doing here?

You see, if Jesus is who he said he is, then his question to his followers is piercing, troubling and hopefully convicting to us:

"Why do you call me 'Lord, Lord,' and do not do what I say?" (Luke 6:46)

Your answer ... s? (Because none of us do.)

"Well, Jesus, you're just ... *kind of* ... important to me. I have many other things competing for that top spot of importance."

"I am lazy."

"I really do not believe what you say, Jesus. Oh, I believe *in you*; but not your promises."

Or perhaps what most will have to say on that fateful day, standing before Jesus:

"I didn't realize it back then, Jesus, Son of God, but I guess I did not really care. Obviously you just were not that important to me."

Oh my.

Jesus deserves your all, your very best, your total commitment, your complete focus. He understands you have a life full of spinning plates, and yet he calls you to,

"But seek first his kingdom and his righteousness, and all these things will be given to you as well." (Matthew 6:33)

Grace is getting what you do not deserve. I certainly do not deserve Jesus. But Jesus absolutely deserves all of me.

Does he you?

---

[1] Mere Christianity (With slight paraphrasing)
[2] C.S. Lewis (With slight paraphrasing)
If you want Lewis' actual words:

I am trying here to prevent anyone saying the really foolish thing that people often say about Him: I'm ready to accept Jesus as a great moral teacher, but I don't accept his claim to be God.

That is the one thing we must not say. A man who was merely a man and said the sort of things Jesus said would not be a great moral teacher. He would either be a lunatic — on the level with the man who says he is a poached egg — or else he would be the Devil of Hell.

You must make your choice. Either this man was, and is, the Son of God, or else a madman or something worse. You can shut him up for a fool, you can spit at him and kill him as a demon or you can fall at his feet and call him Lord and God, but let us not come with any patronizing nonsense about his being a great human teacher. He has not left that open to us. He did not intend to. — _C.S. Lewis Mere Christianity_

118

Salt & Light

As Jesus transitions from his Beatitudes into the depth of the Sermon on the Mount, he makes a declaration:

> "You are the salt of the earth. ...You are the light of the world." (Matthew 5:13-14)

What jumps out at me is his statement of fact: "You are." Not, "I want you to be." Not, "I hope you will be." Not, "Try to be." No ... "You are." Jesus makes a similar declaration just before he ascends to be with the Father:

> "... and you will be my witnesses in Jerusalem and in all Judea and Samaria, and to the ends of the earth." (Acts 1:8)

We must conclude that if we are Christians, if we profess to follow Jesus as our Lord and Savior, then we have no choice: we are salt and we are light, and we are his witnesses. The unresolved questions are, "Are we salty or bland? Are we a bright light or a dim light? And therefore, are we good, positive witnesses for Jesus, or not?

Let me say it a different way: "If you were arrested for being a Christian, a true follower of Jesus, would there be enough evidence to convict you?" In essence, would there be any salt and light? Would there be any fruit? Or would you look like everyone around you, and easily escape conviction?

To help you think about how you might answer this question, let me pose three others:

If I told you Joe Jones was a great running back for his football team, what "evidence" would I present to make my case? The short answer: his statistics – his yards per carry, his average yards per game, his total yards. Perhaps his pass–catching stats.

But if I said he was a great teammate, the evidence would take on a different nature, wouldn't it? Now the answer would not be so much about his stats, but about who he is as a person, and as a teammate – his salt and light.

The evidence now would be more like: He makes everyone around him better. He encourages his teammates. He is selfless. He is a leader, yes, but also a servant leader. He loves his teammates, and they know it. He is always ready to help. He excels in adversity.

Which would you prefer?

But what if I said Joe Jones was a great quarterback? How does this change the evidence? Think about that for a moment. Of course his stats would be important. If he is indeed a great QB, then he will have great stats. But it would not stop there, would it? A great QB would also exhibit the other qualities we listed for a great teammate.

He would have the stats, but he would have so much more.

Now let's revisit your answer as to what evidence could be presented to convict you of being a Christian, someone who is salt and light. Would you want it to be about your stats? Would you present your resume of activities: Church, community, and all that? Imagine sitting in the witness stand and the evidence is all, and only, about your activities. Would you feel comfortable?

Or might you recall Jesus' response to the people who presented him with their stats, their resumes of good deeds?

> "Many will say to me on that day, 'Lord, Lord, did we not prophesy in your name and in your name drive out demons and in your name perform many miracles?' Then I will tell them plainly, 'I never knew you. Away from me, you evildoers!' (Matt. 7:22-23)

I want to be salt and light for Jesus because of who he is – my Lord and Savior, and my best friend – and what he has done for me. I can never repay him, nor can I earn all the love and grace he has lavished on me. I cannot earn it, but I can return it.

I want to 'do' all I can for Jesus and his kingdom, but even more so I want to 'be' Jesus' great teammate.

How?

119

How to be Salt & Light

In his Sermon on the Mount, after his Beatitudes and before he launches into the meat of his talk, Jesus tells his followers:

> "You are the salt of the earth. ...You are the light of the world." (Matthew 5:13-14)

Last week we finished with the question, "How to be salt & light?" Now, I do not want to list ways to be salt and light, because we as humans, and especially us can-do Americans, love a checklist. "Just give me a list and by golly I can, and I will check off all the boxes."

But this is not the way of the Master. He is not about performance and checklists, he is about the heart. So instead, as I contemplated how to talk about being and doing salt & light, four passages came to mind:

> Be wise in the way you act toward outsiders; make the most of every opportunity. **6** Let your conversation be always full of grace, seasoned with salt, so that you may know how to answer everyone. (Colossians 4:5-6)

> ... so that in every way they will make the teaching about God our Savior attractive ... (Titus 2:10)

Praise be to the God and Father of our Lord Jesus Christ, the Father of compassion and the God of all comfort, **4** who comforts us in all our troubles, so that we can comfort those in any trouble with the comfort we ourselves receive from God. (2 Corinthians 1:3-4)

But in your hearts set apart Christ as Lord. And if anyone asks about the hope living within you, always be ready to explain your faith, but with gentleness and respect. 1 Peter 3:15-16   (NIV & TPT)

Imagine those whom you encountered throughout each day coming away thinking:

- "He was so positive and encouraging. He seemed to overflow with warmth and grace. Yes, he did season some truth into our conversation, but that was okay, because he was not at all judgmental. I want what he has." (Colossians 4:5-6)

- "She makes Jesus' teachings and way of life attractive; and Jesus himself warm and welcoming. I don't know, there was just something about her. A light. Yes, that's it, she just seemed to shine with a bright light of life. It is my first time encountering a Christian who actually makes Jesus seem attractive. I want what she has." (Titus 2:10)

- "Life was upside down for me; I was really in a ditch. He reached out to me when it felt like everyone else was avoiding me. As we talked I realized he had experienced challenges and made mistakes just like me. I felt this sense of comfort come over me. I want what he has." (2 Corinthians 1:3-4)

- "Did I tell you about approaching Sallie and asking her why she seemed to have so much peace, as well as so much positive energy? I have noticed this for a while now, and I wanted to know why, because I want what she has. She was gentle and respectful in her response, but she was also very straightforward.

- "She said her hope – her confident expectation – was in Jesus, not others, or a boyfriend or husband, or anything the world has to offer. She even said Jesus was her best friend. Best friend? I had never thought of Jesus that way. Jesus as my best friend? Now that is attractive!" (1 Peter 3:15-16)

Being full of grace, seasoned with salt, makes the gospel attractive. Comforting others with the comfort we have received from Jesus, and being ready to speak boldly about our relationship with Jesus, but doing so with gentleness and respect – now that is salt and light!

No lists, just heart.

120

Headstones

The rabbi asks the Roman soldier to come to his home each morning and ask him these two questions before the rabbi started his day: "Who are you? What are you doing here?"

The rabbi wants to be intentional and proactive about his daily purpose—and so do I—so his story, and my story, are not mostly about the temporal, but instead more about the eternal.

Dallas Willard put it bluntly: "If what you are doing is not eternally significant, then it is eternally insignificant."

That stings, doesn't it?

But if you can answer the second question, "What are you doing here?", with matters of eternal significance, if even just for a part of each day—growing closer to Jesus, seeking him first, making a positive difference in someone's life—showing them Jesus in you (even if unintentionally), then the answer for the, "Who are you?" question will be,

> "Well done, good and faithful servant! You have been faithful with a few things; I will put you in charge of many things. Come and share your master's happiness!"
> (Matt. 25:21)

Friday I was sitting under the excellent teaching of Jeff Miller, the Rector for St. Phillips Anglican Church in Charleston. He was teaching on Ecclesiastes, which is all about the rabbi's two questions. Jeff told the story of walking through the graveyard of his former church and studying the headstones. He came upon an engraving that stated only, "The Belle of Beaufort."

Jeff decided to inquire about this obviously distinct and apparently uniquely fashionable lady, someone everyone would remember, given such an inscription on her headstone. Her death was in 1965, so surely some of the older members would remember her. But no one, absolutely no one remembered her at all.

The Belle of Beaufort was not The Belle for long.

Later that day Dina and I were walking through one of the many old graveyards[1] in Charleston and I noticed three headstones side by side: Recent, to much older. The writing on the more recent was clearly visible, and I pondered the life of this person. Does what is written here capture the essence of their life? The writing on the next older headstone had faded somewhat. The third was completely smooth and bare. Time and weather had erased the life of the entombed.

I thought to myself, "This is what the inheritance we leave behind looks like. It may be 'readable' for a while, but eventually it fades away." It is erased by time and weather. But if we leave a legacy, time nor weather can erase it. Remember: Inheritance is something you leave for someone. Legacy is what you leave in someone.

Just a block or so later I noticed several headstones leaning up against the side of a church, in a dirty side yard, totally abandoned. They looked like the ghosts of eternally insignificant lives.

Oh my.

It is not what is written on your headstone that will matter, it is what you write into the hearts and lives of those around you.

Who are you? What are you doing here?

---

[1] A fun fact: A 'graveyard' is on the grounds of a church. A 'cemetery' stands alone.

Made in the USA
Columbia, SC
19 January 2025

52089983R00252